"I've walked through darkness,
lost in the shadows of my mind,
where fears lurked in every corner
and anxiety clouded my thoughts.
Some days felt eternal,
others passed in a blur
of nameless worries.
But today,
I choose
to see
the
light."

Celeste Leroi

---



First edition - June 2025. No part of this publication may be reproduced, distributed, or transmitted in any form or by any means without the written permission of the author.

For the longest time, I kept my pain to myself, crushed by judgments that branded me as crazy or weak. I was afraid people would dismiss my struggles as "overreacting", so instead of speaking, I shut myself away in silence. In that quiet space, where spoken words failed me, I turned to writing.

That deep sense of not fitting in, of being somehow different - I've been there too. But here's the thing: these feelings are far more universal than we realize.

You're not fighting this battle alone. This book was born from breaking that silence, creating a space to put words to our shared struggles and hopes. Because yes, there is a way forward. In these pages, I hope you'll find words that make you feel understood and less alone. And since sometimes words aren't enough to quiet our minds, you'll find coloring pages scattered throughout. Coloring is an invitation to let go, to give your anxious thoughts a break. It's a gentle way to anchor yourself in the present moment, focusing only on each stroke of color.

This isn't about pushing away your pain, it's about embracing it to move through it. Think of this book as opening a window to your soul: approach it with curiosity, kindness, and hope for brighter days ahead.

A little optimism can light up even the darkest corners of our minds.

# Why Are You Here?

You're holding this book, maybe out of curiosity, maybe because you're searching for answers. But have you taken a moment to ask yourself why you're really here? What's driving you to seek understanding and change?

**What are you looking to change in your life?**

.................................................................

.................................................................

.................................................................

**What's at the root of your struggles?**

.................................................................

.................................................................

.................................................................

**Can you put a name to the negative feeling or emotion that's taking over?**

.................................................................

.................................................................

.................................................................

**Are you ready to explore ideas that might push you outside your comfort zone?**

.................................................................

.................................................................

**How do you feel about exploring parts of yourself that you haven't faced before?**

.................................................................

.................................................................

# Table of Contents

# From Fear to Anxiety

*Picture yourself at the edge of a cliff, the wind blows through your hair, your feet just inches from the edge. Your heart races, hands get sweaty, and a shiver runs down your spine. That's fear. A primal emotion, a warning signal that guided our ancestors through prehistoric dangers and now keeps you from jumping.* But today, fear isn't limited to physical threats. It pops up in your daily life, like during an important presentation or a tough conversation.

At its most basic, fear is there to protect you. When it kicks in, your brain sends warning signals, flooding your body with adrenaline.

Your breathing quickens, your muscles tense, preparing you to "fight or flee", getting you ready to face danger or escape from it. **But what happens when this fear has nowhere to go?**

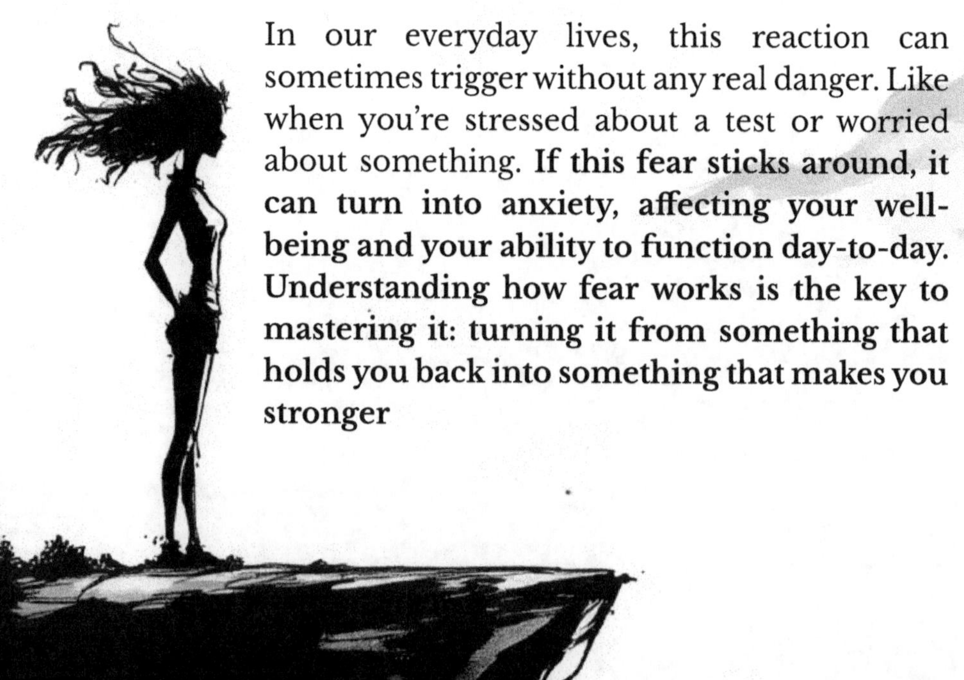

In our everyday lives, this reaction can sometimes trigger without any real danger. Like when you're stressed about a test or worried about something. **If this fear sticks around, it can turn into anxiety, affecting your well-being and your ability to function day-to-day. Understanding how fear works is the key to mastering it: turning it from something that holds you back into something that makes you stronger**

# Dictionary definition of anxiety:

Anxiety n. A distressing feeling of worry and fear about what might happen; a state of mental tension.

## The raw truth about anxiety:

Anxiety is like a cold fist squeezing your heart. Making you feel dizzy and unsteady every time you face a decision. It sneaks into the quiet moments, stretching seconds into hours, turning hours into endless days filled with worry. It's the tightness in your chest, the overwhelming feeling that hits you out of nowhere, weighing so heavy on your shoulders that it slows your steps and drains your energy. Anxiety is that nagging voice in your head that won't shut up, questioning everything you do, every word you say, every moment of silence.

It leaves you exhausted, struggling to find peace in a mind that won't stop racing with doubt and fear. It's a daily battle that no one else can see, fighting against fears only you can feel.

# Anxiety happens when fear spreads beyond right now

Fear transforms into anxiety when you stop worrying about immediate threats and start obsessing over endless "what if" scenarios. When you start expecting the worst from future events or uncertain situations.

<u>Let's go back to our first example:</u>
*You're standing at the edge of a cliff, wind blowing through your hair... and a shiver runs down your spine.* But this time, you're safely strapped into a bungee cord, surrounded by professional guides ensuring your safety.

Even though you're completely safe, your mind is crowded with "what if" thoughts and worst-case scenarios. Yeah, jumping off a cliff feels completely unnatural. Most people don't jump right away, fear takes over, but your mind works overtime to convince your subconscious that there's no real danger. You'll jump, scream, and end up loving it... And if you don't like it, you've learned something about yourself. Either way, you come out stronger.

The same goes for anxiety: Your mind, your instincts put you on high alert. It's impossible to relax or think about anything else but that negative thought taking over. It's up to you, and only you, to convince yourself that the outcome isn't as dramatic as it seems.

Understanding the difference between fear and anxiety is like switching on a light in a dark room. It might not chase away all the shadows right away, but it helps you see things more clearly.

Anxiety doesn't dim your inner light; it makes you cherish every glimmer.

**Fear comes whether you want it or not.**

You constantly doubt yourself, wondering if you're overreacting. *"Am I making a big deal out of nothing?"* It feels so intense that you search for solid reasons to justify what you're feeling.

Stop.

Your anxiety is real and valid; you don't need anyone's permission to feel what you feel. Your fears, however irrational they might seem, are part of your reality. Your pain matters, even when no one can see it.

What you're going through is real. Your feelings are valid. Your experiences, messy and complicated as they are, matter.

Anxiety turns everyday situations into threats. It flips your world upside down, making simple tasks feel impossible. This isn't your fault, and you shouldn't feel guilty about it. Your struggle is real, even if others can't see it.

When you stop fighting and accept that it as part of your life right now, you'll begin to find some peace.

# When Anxiety Takes Over

If you've experienced these sensations or symptoms, it could be a sign that you're dealing with anxiety:

## *Physical Manifestations:*

☐ **Difficulty Breathing:** Each breath becomes a struggle, as if the air itself is fighting against you.

☐ **Muscle Tension:** Your shoulders, neck, back – your entire body turns to concrete, stiff and painful, refusing to relax.

☐ **Cold Sweats or Hot Flashes:** Waves of heat alternate with icy chills out of nowhere.

☐ **Chest Pain:** That crushing tightness in your chest that stops you in your tracks.

☐ **Dizziness:** The world around you becomes unstable, as if the ground is shifting beneath your feet.

☐ **Heart Palpitations:** Your heart races in your chest, beating so hard you think it might jump out.

☐ **Metallic Taste:** A strange metallic taste fills your mouth.

☐ **Derealization:** Sometimes, you feel like you're watching your own life from the outside, detached from your body.

# How Anxiety Affects Your Body

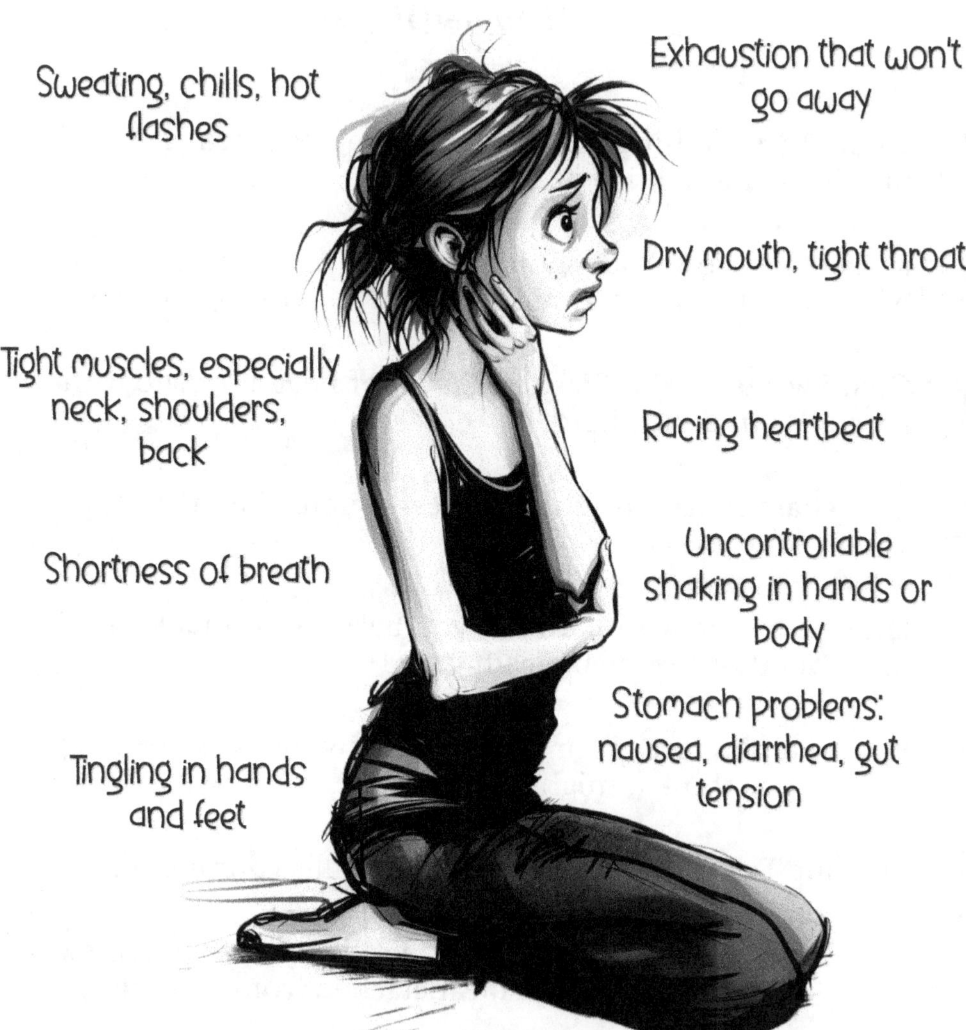


Anxiety's physical effects are often underestimated; in about 70% of consultations for unexplained pain, anxiety frequently plays a significant role.

<u>*Psychological and Behavioral Signs:*</u>

☐ **Sleep Problems:** You lie awake at night overthinking everything, your mind refusing to shut down.

☐ **Feeling Drained:** A bone-deep tiredness that doesn't go away, even after sleeping.

☐ **Trouble Focusing:** Your mind jumps everywhere, making it impossible to concentrate on one thing.

☐ **On High Alert:** You startle easily at the smallest sounds or movements, your senses constantly scanning for danger.

☐ **Dodging Situations:** You go out of your way to avoid anything that might trigger your anxiety.

☐ **Overthinking :** You analyze conversations over and over, thinking of what you should have said.

☐ **Worst-Case Thinking:** Minor problems quickly snowball into disasters in your mind.

☐ **Stuck Thoughts:** Unwanted ideas get stuck on repeat in your head and refuse to leave.

☐ **On Edge:** You feel irritable and tense most of the time, like you might snap at any moment.

# How Are You Really Doing?

Take a second to check in with yourself. Where do you fall between these feelings?

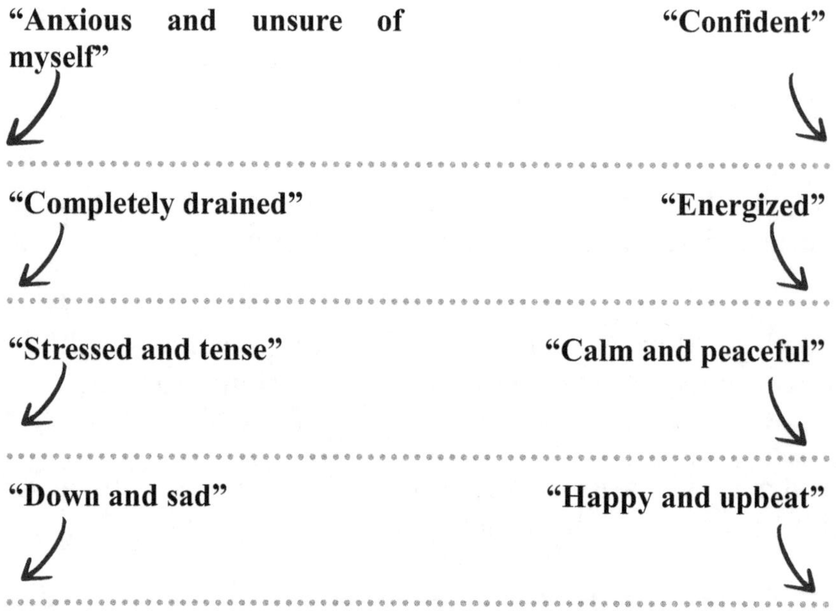

14

What's going through your head right now? Are you stuck in the past, worrying about the future, or actually in the present?

. . . . . . . . . . . . . . . . . . . . . . . . . . . . . . . . . . . . . . . . . . . . . . . . . . .

. . . . . . . . . . . . . . . . . . . . . . . . . . . . . . . . . . . . . . . . . . . . . . . . . . .

. . . . . . . . . . . . . . . . . . . . . . . . . . . . . . . . . . . . . . . . . . . . . . . . . . .

. . . . . . . . . . . . . . . . . . . . . . . . . . . . . . . . . . . . . . . . . . . . . . . . . . .

Is it these thoughts that are messing with your mood, or did something happen recently?

. . . . . . . . . . . . . . . . . . . . . . . . . . . . . . . . . . . . . . . . . . . . . . . . . . .

. . . . . . . . . . . . . . . . . . . . . . . . . . . . . . . . . . . . . . . . . . . . . . . . . . .

. . . . . . . . . . . . . . . . . . . . . . . . . . . . . . . . . . . . . . . . . . . . . . . . . . .

. . . . . . . . . . . . . . . . . . . . . . . . . . . . . . . . . . . . . . . . . . . . . . . . . . .

We all have fears that hold us back. What's getting in your way right now, and how are you dealing with it day to day?

. . . . . . . . . . . . . . . . . . . . . . . . . . . . . . . . . . . . . . . . . . . . . . . . . . .

. . . . . . . . . . . . . . . . . . . . . . . . . . . . . . . . . . . . . . . . . . . . . . . . . . .

. . . . . . . . . . . . . . . . . . . . . . . . . . . . . . . . . . . . . . . . . . . . . . . . . . .

. . . . . . . . . . . . . . . . . . . . . . . . . . . . . . . . . . . . . . . . . . . . . . . . . . .

When's the last time you felt this fear, and what did you do about it?

. . . . . . . . . . . . . . . . . . . . . . . . . . . . . . . . . . . . . . . . . . . . . . . . . . .

. . . . . . . . . . . . . . . . . . . . . . . . . . . . . . . . . . . . . . . . . . . . . . . . . . .

. . . . . . . . . . . . . . . . . . . . . . . . . . . . . . . . . . . . . . . . . . . . . . . . . . .

. . . . . . . . . . . . . . . . . . . . . . . . . . . . . . . . . . . . . . . . . . . . . . . . . . .

Which part of you feels like it's walking around without armor right now? How is this showing up when you deal with people or make decisions?

Is there something about yourself you're not ready to face?

If so, why not? What's the worst that could happen if you got real with yourself?

Can you actually back up what you just said with evidence?

# My Anxiety Triggers:

- [ ] **Highway Driving**: Freaking out about crashes, getting lost, or going too fast.

- [ ] **Phone Calls**: The panic of calling people, especially strangers—afraid I'll stutter or sound stupid.

- [ ] **Grocery Shopping**: That overwhelmed feeling when the store is packed.

- [ ] **Waiting for Answers or Updates**: The anxiety of waiting for an important phone call or news from a loved one.

- [ ] **Public Transit**: Crowds, delays, unfamiliar routes: total anxiety factories.

- [ ] **People Stuff**: Dreading conflict, never knowing how to say no, getting nervous before hangouts.

- [ ] **Doctor's Visits**: The anxiety spike before appointments or just talking to medical people.

- [ ] **Hearing About Someone Sick or Dying**: It can remind you of life's fragility and spark anxiety.

- [ ] **Being Far From Safety**: Panicking when I'm nowhere near home or a hospital.

- [ ] **Coffee**: That caffeine buzz that feels exactly like anxiety kicking in.

- [ ] **Certain Sounds or Lights**: They hit different when you're already on edge, like sensory overload.

# The day anxiety kept me from seeing my friends

Yet another invitation turned down, yet another excuse made up. You wish you could tell them it's not personal, that sometimes anxiety drowns out the longing to connect.

Apology texts pile up on your phone. In their minds, it's simple: you're pulling away. They can't grasp that paralysis that freezes you at the doorstep.

Avoiding these situations becomes your armour, your go-to response. But each time you back away, the next outing gets even harder, until even the simplest social gathering becomes overwhelming.

The solution isn't forcing yourself into uncomfortable situations, but taking baby steps at your own pace. Start small with quiet settings and familiar places. A chill coffee shop instead of a noisy bar. A quick walk in the park rather than a full-blown party.

Most importantly, open up to your close friends about what you're dealing with, not everything at once, just whatever you're comfortable sharing. Real friends don't need to fully understand to fully show up.

Not sure how to start that conversation? Here's a simple exercise to help you out.

# Have you ever talked about this with friends or family?

This exercise is designed to guide you step by step through the tough but important process of opening up about your anxiety to someone you trust. It'll help you organize your thoughts, clarify your needs, and navigate the conversation (before, during, and after) so you can build stronger emotional support.

**What am I ready to share about my anxiety and struggles?**

**What I want to say to them:**

*Tip: Use real-life examples to make your feelings relatable.*

**What I need them to understand:**

**How my loved ones can support me:**

**How we can better understand each other:**

......................................................................

......................................................................

......................................................................

*Encourage them to ask questions and share their own feelings too.*

**Notes on their reactions and how the conversation went:**

......................................................................

......................................................................

......................................................................

......................................................................

......................................................................

......................................................................

......................................................................

......................................................................

......................................................................

......................................................................

......................................................................

These reactions aren't just about you, they also reflect how your loved ones view anxiety (and sometimes their lack of understanding). It's a reminder that relationships are messy, and everyone filters things through their own lens..

# Common unhelpful responses they might throw at you:

"JUST TOUGH IT OUT."

"YOU'RE OVERREACTING."

"STOP STRESSING OVER NOTHING."

"IT'S ALL IN YOUR HEAD."

"CALM DOWN, YOU'LL BE FINE."

"EVERYONE FEELS LIKE THIS SOMETIMES—YOU'LL GET OVER IT."

"YOU'RE JUST SEEKING ATTENTION."

"YOU ALWAYS MAKE EVERYTHING A BIG DEAL."

"OTHER PEOPLE HAVE REAL PROBLEMS."

"JUST STOP THINKING ABOUT IT."

"IT'S BECAUSE OF YOUR NEGATIVE ATTITUDE…"

"Please understand I don't choose this. It's a weight I'm trying to carry and manage every day. I don't need you to fix me. I just need:

Your support, not your criticism,

Your curiosity, not quick fixes,

Your listening ear, not your judgment."

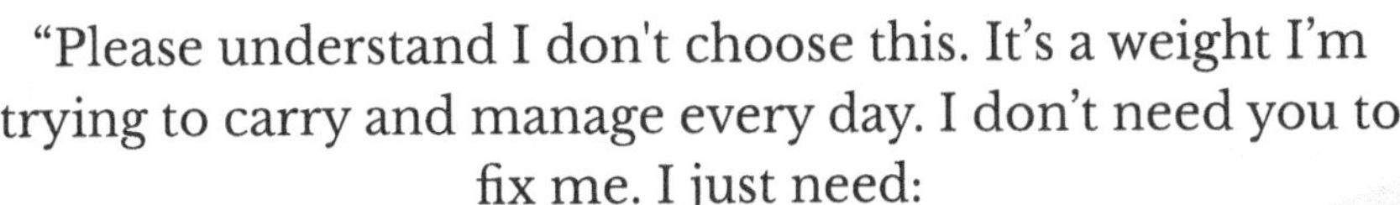

# I wish I could read people's minds.

How much of your day is spent scripting imaginary dialogues, playing out fake conversations that'll never happen? This isn't just overthinking, it's mental time travel to disasters that don't exist.

That desperate need to predict every reaction is eating you alive. A throwaway comment morphs into a landmine. Silence becomes a courtroom verdict.

Your brain's on permanent red alert, amping up everyday moments into life-or-death situations: A job interview? Public execution. A checkup? A death sentence? Hanging with friends? A social disaster.

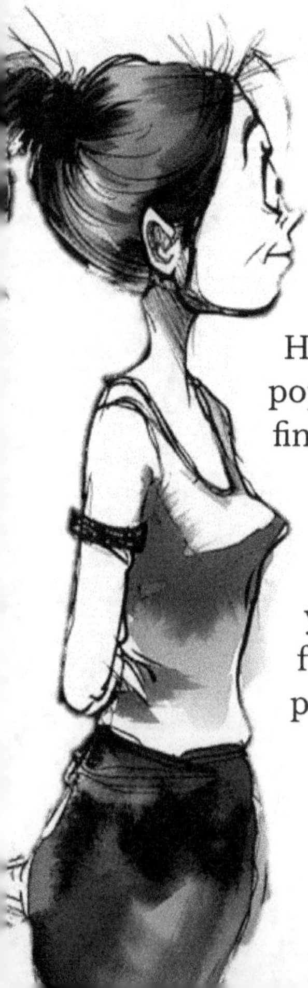

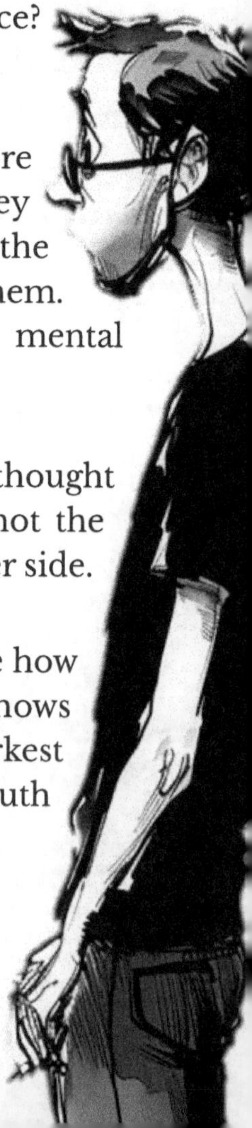

It's a self-feeding cycle. The more you fuel these fears, the bigger they grow. The bigger they grow, the harder you try to anticipate them. Before long, you're stuck in a mental Groundhog Day.

Here's the shift: When a negative thought pops up, treat it like a rough draft, not the final version. Force it to argue the other side.

In the next few pages, we'll explore how to recalibrate a mind that only shows you half the story. Between your darkest fears and rosiest hopes, the truth probably lies somewhere in between.

# The Anxiety Clock

"Hell of a day... I'm running on fumes but already dreading tomorrow. Gonna be another dumpster fire."

1 AM... 2 AM... 3 AM... "How the hell do I handle this? What if I crash and burn?" 4 AM. Cool. "What if I..."

"Not now... I can feel it creeping up. Gotta hold it together. Can't lose it here. Not here. Not in front of them."

"Didn't sleep a wink. Look like hell. How am I supposed to function? I'm already dead on my feet..."

# Turn every worst-case scenario into a hopeful one

Here's your power move: Whenever your brain spins a disaster movie plot, write it in the left column. Then, challenge yourself to draft a **realistic** positive version in the right column. Not a perfect fairytale, just a version where things go... fine.

For example, *"They'll think I'm weird"* / *"They're too busy overthinking their own stuff to notice mine"* or *"Awkward silence incoming?"* / *"Comfortable pauses are normal, not every second needs talking"*

## NEGATIVE HOT TAKE | NEUTRAL/POSITIVE HOT TAKE

Afterward, ask yourself:

Which version **actually played out**?
Wasn't reality usually **somewhere in the middle**?
How many of these "disasters" **ever even happened**?

**<u>Make it a rule</u>:** For every doomsday scenario you write, you *have to* brainstorm a neutral or hopeful alternative. Wrap it up with a tiny action plan for handling the situation. Spoiler: 90% of those catastrophes you're scripting? They'll never make it past draft mode.

*Remember this:* Your brain's a horror movie pro. Time to train it to write rom-coms or chill documentaries.

# Social Anxiety: Why your brain's gaslighting you

Life's full of everyday moments that feel like psychological warfare. A waiting room? Pure torture. A quick "hello" in the elevator? Absolute hell. While everyone else is living their lives, you're stuck in survival mode.

Social anxiety isn't just "shyness". It's the crushing belief that everyone's grading you constantly. You're exhausted from performing "normal"...

**But here's what your anxiety won't tell you:** People aren't scanning you for flaws. They're too busy with their own lives to care about your "awkward" laugh or that thing you said three days ago. That fear of judgment? It's like wearing beer goggles to a job interview. Everything's looks warped.

Your goal isn't to "fix" yourself. It's to exist: messily, unapologetically, fully. So what if they judge you? There's nothing you can do about it, but you can stop handing them the mic. Read this carefully: **Their judgment only has the power you give it.**

Every time you cancel plans to avoid "weirding people out", you're letting their imaginary scorecards win. Every time you push through the discomfort anyway, you're hacking the system. **You're not a character in their story.**

Here are some exercises to overcome your social anxiety:

## Exercise 1: Build your exposure ladder

Pick a social situation that spikes your anxiety. The goal is to break it down into small, manageable steps: from *"I can handle this"* to *"This feels intense".*

*Example: Ordering Coffee at a Café*

1. Scope out the café from outside
2. Grab a to-go order quickly
3. Chat briefly while ordering
4. Sit outside during off-peak hours
5. Stay during busier times
6. People-watch for 10+ minutes

For each step:

- Rate your anxiety (0 = calm – 10 = panic)
- Stay in the situation until your anxiety drops by at least 30%
- Jot down what actually happened (not your fears)
- Move to the next step only when ready (no rushing!)

Why this works:

Every time you face a fear and survive, your brain gets an update: *"Hey, this wasn't life-or-death after all."* Progress isn't just about courage, it's about teaching your brain to stop overestimating danger.

# Exercise 2 : Detox your thinking

Anxiety brain loves to distort reality, it's like wearing foggy glasses that magnify threats and shrink your ability to cope. This exercise helps you wipe the lens clean.

<u>Situation</u> : Briefly describe what happened

<u>Automatic Thought</u> : Ex: *"They think I'm awkward"*

<u>Anxiety Level (0-10)</u> : *[Rate it]*

**Challenge the Script** :

1. **What's my proof?** (Did they actually roll their eyes, or is my anxiety editing the scene?)

2. **Would this hold up in court?** (What hard evidence do I have that this thought is true?)

3. **How would a stranger describe this?** (Hint: They'd probably say you're just... existing.)

4. **Is this thought my ally or my saboteur?**

5. **What's a less dramatic take?** (Ex: Maybe they're distracted, not judging.)

<u>New Perspective:</u> *[Write here]*

<u>New Anxiety Level (0-10):</u> *[Rate again]*

By tracking these thoughts, you start to spot the patterns that keep repeating. You realize they're just thoughts, not facts. This isn't about forced positivity, it's about seeing reality more clearly and more balanced.

## Exercise 3: Daily Micro-Wins

Pick one tiny social action to tackle daily. The goal isn't to crush it—it's to act despite the discomfort.

### Examples:

- Say hi to a stranger
- Ask a cashier a quick question (e.g., *"Is this line for pickup?"*)
- Make a casual comment (e.g., *"Love your shoes!"*)
- Hold eye contact for 3 seconds

### Post-Action Debrief:

- What actually went down
- What surprised you
- One thing you learned

### Rules of the Game:

- Start stupid small
- Move at your own pace
- Celebrate any progress (emoji dance allowed 🕺)
- Perfect isn't the goal: showing up is
- One bad day doesn't delete your wins

Why this works:

Every time you push through a tiny social challenge, you're gathering receipts to prove your anxiety wrong. These micro-wins rewrite your story, from passive victim to active hero of your own growth.

# Beyond Stoicism: The Art of Not Giving a F*ck

Life's a series of choices, and one of the most crucial is deciding **what gets to rent space in your head.**

You get to choose what deserves your attention and energy. So why waste that mental real estate on stuff that, let's be real, doesn't actually matter?

Learning to let go isn't about becoming indifferent or numb. No, it's a form of liberation. When you stop clinging to minor annoyances, other people's judgments, or small failures, you free yourself. You make room for what actually matters: your growth, your well-being, your dreams.

Over time, you'll find that 90% of what felt urgent loses its shine. That's emotional growth at work, inviting you to reconsider what truly deserves your attention, not your neighbor's.

So make choices that align with who you are, not who you're expected to be. And everything else? Well, you can simply choose not to give a f*ck about it.

What "must-dos" in your life are actually "meh-dos"? What "urgent" thing drains your energy but adds zero joy or growth?

Think of a recent frustration. How would your life improve if you stopped letting it rent space in your head?

What judgment from others scares you most? How could you stop letting it define your choices?

What three priorities deserve your focus right now? How can you protect and grow them daily?

What outdated rulebook are you still following "just because"? What societal script are you acting out that doesn't even align with your values?

# The Detachment Decision Tree

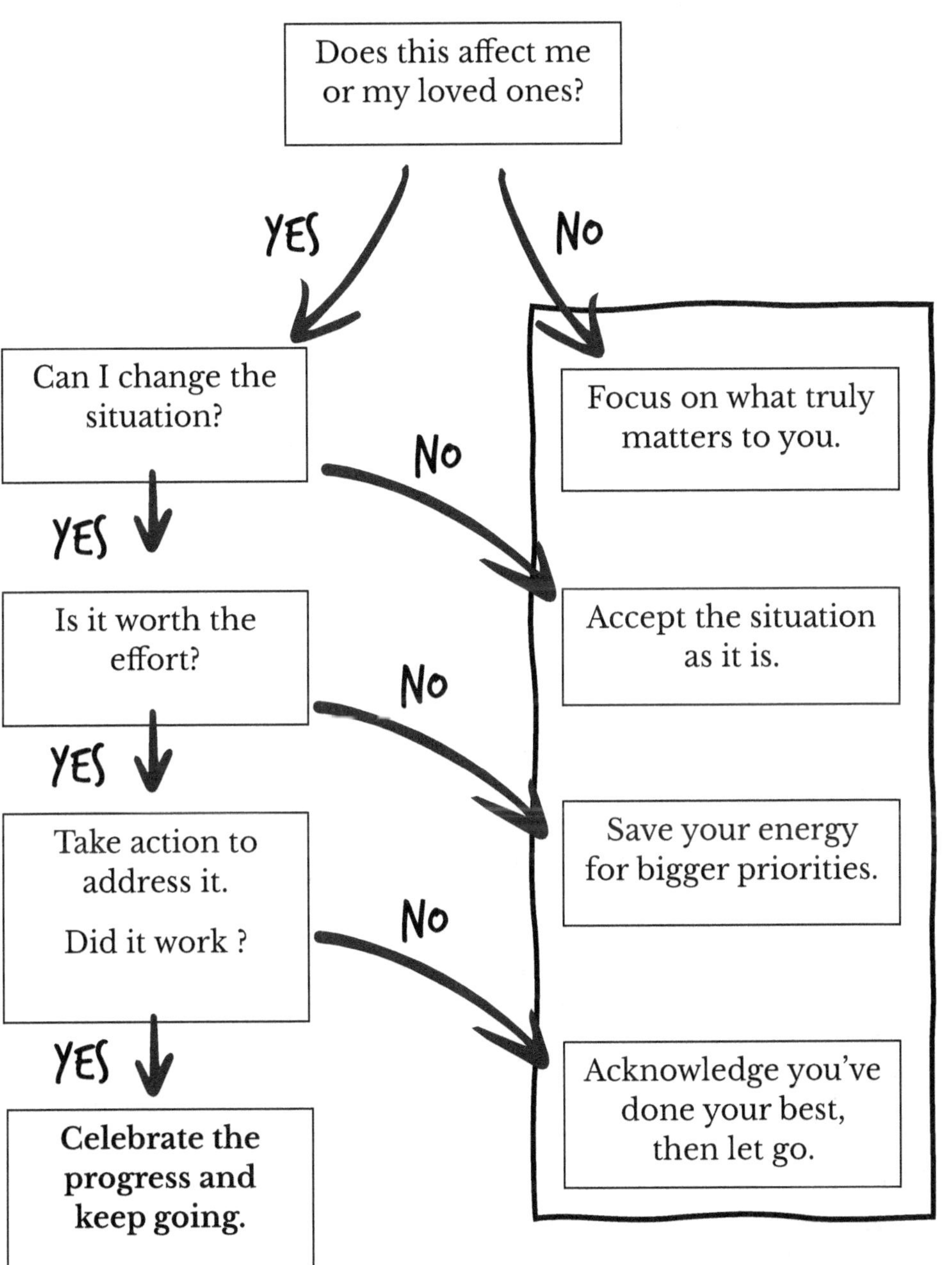

**If you can't be extraordinary, be deeply ordinary.**

Look in the mirror. Who do you see? Someone exhausted from chasing society's hustle culture ideals of "exceptional"? **Pause.** Life isn't about winning some never-ending rat race to "extraordinary".

That relentless grind for perfection, comparing yourself to Instagram-perfect lives and unattainable standards, isn't ambition. **It's toxic pressure.** A game where you're constantly losing to imaginary competitors.

And let's talk social media: Your wins feel invisible next to everyone else's "best of" montage. That comparison trap? It's gaslighting you into believing you're failing at life, sabotaging your confidence, relationships, and right to just... be happy.

**But here's the truth bomb:** So what if you're not "extraordinary"? Since when did that become the price tag for happiness? Is life only worth living if it's grand and spectacular? Would you somehow be worthless if you never reached those heights? **Hell no.**

These questions aren't meant to shame you, they're here to expose the gap between society's script and your peace. Start seeing the value in your own path. True fulfillment isn't about being the main character in someone else's story. It's about owning your messy, imperfect, human journey.

Get real.
Be unapologetically
you.

**No one will care about :**

- Your lipstick shade of the week.
- How many designer bags you own.
- Your perfectly curated profile pic.
- Your Instagram follower count.
- The letters after your name.
- That one rogue pimple you're obsessing over.


**What they will remember :**

- The time you actually showed up for them.
- How you made them feel.
- Whether you kept your promises.
- If they could count on you when it mattered.
- The way you treated them, even when no one was watching.
- The quiet, lasting impact you had on their life.

The True Wealth of Lakshmi

Lakshmi, the Hindu goddess of wealth
and prosperity, both material and
spiritual, is revered for her generosity
and ability to bring fortune.

# The true wealth of Lakshmi

In Mumbai, there lived a self-made businessman named Ravi. He'd built his empire from the ground up but worried his daughter Diya, raised in luxury, might never grasp the value of their privileged life. One day, he took her to the city's impoverished neighborhoods, far from their gated community. The streets buzzed with life, families crowded into modest homes, and children played with makeshift toys.

On their drive home, Ravi asked:

"So, what did you think of today?"

"It was... eye-opening", Diya replied.

"Did you see how people here live?"

"I did", she said. "I saw they're surrounded by friends, while we're surrounded by staff. They sleep together as a family while I sleep alone in my room. We have books to learn from, they have stories to share. We have guards for security, they protect each other as neighbors. We have fancy toys, they have imagination. Our dining table seats twenty but keeps us apart. Their one pot of food brings them closer."

Ravi was speechless, realizing that the lesson he had planned to teach had become a lesson for himself.

Then, with a smile, Diya concluded:

"Thank you, Dad, for showing me all the things we're missing."

**This story reminds us that gratitude and contentment are priceless treasures, often buried under our endless chase for what we don't have.**

That voice telling you you're not good enough? It didn't just pop up overnight. It's rooted in childhood , every careless comment from our loved ones carved a groove in your brain.

*"You're useless", "How are you this bad at everything?", "This is all your fault"* stacked up over time. Now, they're the broken record playing in your head, judging you 24/7.

**You're stuck in a tug-of-war:** Part of you wants to live authentically. The other part is desperate for approval. So you shrink. You say "yes" when you mean "no". You apologize for existing. Slowly, you become a stranger to yourself.

Your brain becomes a failure magnifier. Wins get dismissed like spam emails. Mistakes? They're bolded, highlighted, saved forever. This imbalance fuels your anxiety, digging deeper each day. But here's the thing: That distorted lens isn't permanent.

Truth is, you're way more capable than your inner critic admits. Others see your strengths clearly, it's you who struggles to claim them. Together, we'll bridge the gap between how you see yourself and how the world actually sees you.

# The clarity window

When self-esteem runs low, your brain becomes a funhouse mirror, distorting how you see yourself. You might:

- Downplay your strengths (like they're no big deal)
- Zoom in on flaws (hello, microscope mode)
- Assume everyone's judging your "weak spots"
- Brush off compliments (as if they're spam)

Time to fact-check your inner critic:

Write down 3 "absolute truths" you believe about yourself. Examples: *"I'm awkward", "I'm not good enough", "People think I'm boring".*
For each "truth", ask:

- **Is this always true?** (Like, 100% of the time?)
- **Where did this script come from?**
  A specific moment?
  A vague feeling?
- **Has anyone ever contradicted this?**
  (What'd they say?)
- **Would I let my best friend talk about themselves this way?**

Notice what comes up:

**Defensiveness** (*"But my case is different!"*)
**Aha moments** (*"Huh... maybe it's not that black-and-white."*)
**Discomfort** (*"Why does questioning this feel so weird?"*)

**Goal:** This isn't about proving you wrong, it's about showing you that your self-image is just one interpretation, not an absolute truth.

# Digging up the roots of self-doubt

Low self-esteem is built over years of experiences, words, and side-eyes. These questions will help you unpack the baggage.

*The Script You Inherited*

- What behaviors were you constantly criticized for growing up?
- What did "success" look like in your family?
- When did you first learn to obsess over others opinions?
- What moment made you start questioning your worth?
- What childhood passions made you feel truly alive, and have you buried them?

*Your Survival Tactics*

- When you shrink in groups, what judgment are you dodging?
- What's the worst-case scenario if you actually showed up as your full self?
- What armor do you wear daily, and what's it really protecting?
- How does fear of criticism steer your decisions?

*Your Relationship with You*

- What self-judgment cuts the deepest?
- What part of yourself feels "too much" or "not enough" and why?
- What would you tell your childhood self if they walked in right now?
- What hidden strengths are you ready to finally claim?

**Remember:** Unpacking these patterns helps you rewrite the rules.

# Track your reactions

Your daily interactions are mirrors, they reflect how you see yourself and others. For each scenario below, jot down:

- **Your gut reaction** (first thought)
- **Your emotional vibe** (anxious? proud? irritated?)
- **What you usually do**
- (people-please? shut down? speak up?)

**Scenarios to unpack:**

1. Someone compliments you
2. You're asked to speak in a group
3. You need to ask for help
4. You nail something important
5. You mess up
6. Someone criticizes you
7. You disagree with others
8. You get promoted

**The Debrief:**

**When do you feel rock-solid?** (What strengths shine here?)

**When do you self-sabotage?** (What stories are you telling yourself?)

**How do others come across in these moments?** (Allies? critics? NPCs?)

**Why this works:**

Confident moments = clues to your hidden superpowers. Self-doubt spirals = red flags for limiting beliefs.

And how you view others? It'll show whether their opinions empower or control you.

Use this check-in to rewrite the script.

# The Art of Being Yourself

In a cramped Paris apartment lived Sarah, an artist shackled by self-doubt. Each morning, she'd stare at her half-finished canvases, frozen by the fear that nothing she made would ever be enough. Her studio, once a creative sanctuary, had become a gilded cage overflowing with abandoned dreams.

One day, her elderly neighbor Madame Chen knocked on her door, her crinkled eyes sparkling. Clutched in her shaky hands was a painting Sarah had tossed in the trash the night before.

"May I?" Madame Chen asked, nodding toward the cluttered room. Sarah flushed but gestured her inside.

"Why discard this?" The old woman propped the canvas on a dusty easel.

"It's not good enough", Sarah muttered. "None of them are."

Madame Chen's smile deepened as she pulled a tarnished hand mirror from her bag. "Look", she urged. "What do you see?"

"Flaws", Sarah shot back.

"Now, close your eyes", Mrs. Chen continued. "When you think of yourself painting, how do you feel?"

Sarah paused. "Free. Alive. Like... like the world disappears."

"That is your beauty", the woman whispered. "Creation isn't about perfection; it's about leaving your fingerprints on the world. These 'flaws'?" She tapped the mirror.

"They're proof you showed up."

She thrust Sarah's most battered paintbrush into her hands. "Now feel, don't think."

For the first time in years, Sarah painted wildly, guided by raw emotion. The result wasn't polished, but it pulsed with messy, magnificent life.

Today, Sarah's art doesn't beg for approval. It demands truth. Because radiant beauty blooms from broken places, just as stars only burn bright against the dark.

The mirror doesn't just reflect our faces, it captures the stories we tell ourselves. What if the voice that constantly finds your flaws isn't telling the truth? What if, beneath the anxiety and self-criticism, your authentic self is waiting to create something only you can bring to life?

# The Control Paradox

Control. That word silently sets the rhythm of your days. You seek it everywhere, in your routines, your to-do lists, your endless mental rehearsals of "what-if" scenarios. This relentless chase for control? It's your shield against uncertainty, your way of armoring up against life's chaos.

The real paradox? The control you crave quietly cages you. It traps you in a tight comfort zone, blocking opportunities that could rewrite your story. Every new situation feels threatening. Every change seems risky.

So start small. Make one decision that scares you just a little, and see what happens. Every choice, even a tiny one, becomes a stepping stone to a more alive version of your life.

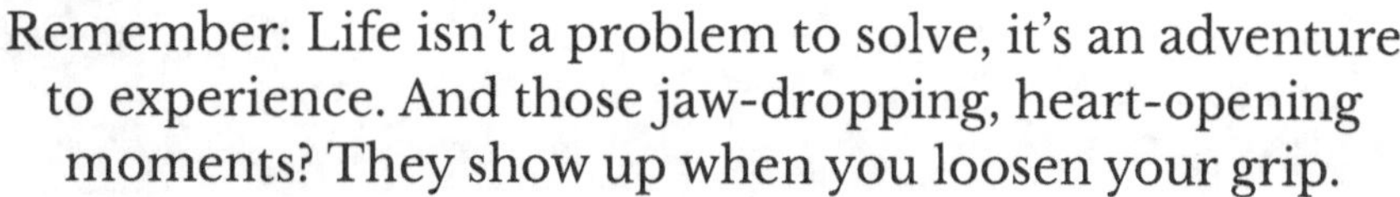

Remember: Life isn't a problem to solve, it's an adventure to experience. And those jaw-dropping, heart-opening moments? They show up when you loosen your grip.

What have you sacrificed to keep up the illusion of control in your life? Was it worth it?

What parts of your identity or past are fueling your need to control everything?

What are you afraid of losing if you let go?

How have your fears of failure and the unknown shaped your past decisions?

What experiences have you avoided because of uncertainty and how could they actually help you grow?

**What's one thing about yourself you could change to move forward?**

**Besides yourself, who or what's holding you back?**

Some days feel heavier than they look.
The world blurs, and every step feels
like it leads nowhere.

Doubt thickens the air. Not loud just steady,
like a whisper you can't shake.
You wonder if the fog will ever lift.

You try to move forward,
but everything feels like waiting.
Waiting to feel better.
Waiting to be sure.
Waiting to know where you're going.

Even in the stillness, you're not stuck.
Even lost, you're learning.
Even slow, you're moving.

This fog? It isn't forever.
It teaches you to listen differently—
to your breath,
to your strength,
to the faint pulse of hope beneath it all.

And when the light returns,
you'll see that you weren't broken.
You were just becoming.

Let's play with a ridiculous scenario: what if you could predict and control every single aspect of your life with absolute certainty? Imagine a world where every event, every encounter, every conversation was 100% predictable. Sounds pretty comforting at first glance, right?

But dig a little deeper:

**How would you make decisions if you already knew every outcome?**

**How would it feel to have no surprises?**

*Say you knew your future was already picture-perfect. Everything's going to work out great.*

Where's the incentive to grow, learn, or push yourself? Our motivation typically comes from wanting to achieve something meaningful or overcome a challenge, it's hardwired into our need for growth and accomplishment.

Similarly, if happiness were a sure thing, would you even appreciate it? Would you laugh at jokes if you already knew the punchline?

Flip the script: What if your future looked like a nightmare? Would you just sit back and wait for disaster?

This whole thought experiment is meant to help you realize that uncertainty doesn't just bring worst-case scenarios. There's one thing you can absolutely count on: every action has a result, good or bad. It's entirely up to you to learn from it, grow through it, experiment, and reinvent yourself.

**Check the areas where you crave control (or fear losing it):**

**DAILY LIFE :**

☐ Routines & rituals

☐ Personal organization

☐ Budget & finances

☐ Time management

**WORK :**

☐ Job performance

☐ Approval from bosses/clients

☐ Work-life balance

☐ Projects & deadlines

**RELATIONSHIPS :**

☐ Your romantic relationship

☐ Family dynamics & expectations

☐ Friendships

☐ Social media interactions

**HEALTH & WELLNESS :**

☐ Sleep habits

☐ Diet & nutrition

☐ Personal or loved ones health

☐ Body image

Which category feels most overwhelming? (Work/school, personal/family life, health, etc.)

# Mapping Your Control Zones

From the areas you checked, pinpoint:

- **The anxiety heavyweight** (Which one spikes your stress the most?)
- **The frequent flyer** (Which one keeps popping up?)
- **The daily disruptor** (Which one hijacks your routine?)

What's your go-to panic move when control slips here?

What's the real fear lurking underneath? How's clinging to control letting you dodge that bullet?

When was the last time you felt loosey-goosey about this? (Think: pre-control obsession era ✬)

What fragile part of you is this "control armor" protecting?

When did you last surprise yourself by handling chaos without micromanaging?

Build your "chill ladder". What's the easiest rung to start climbing?

Don't worry about
where you'll land,
focus on how the
world looks from above

**"I'm stuck between plastering on a smile to hide my anxiety and screaming my pain to the world."**

Do you wake up every day wondering how you'll get through it? That forced smile isn't just a mood—it's survival gear. Your armor, your shield against the chaos.

You wear it to hide your pain, to appear strong, calm, in control. But inside, you're screaming. This constant battle drains you from within, leaving you isolated even in a crowded room..

In relationships, that mask builds walls. *"Do I dare show the real me?"* You're terrified of exposing your vulnerabilities, of being truly seen.

So you double down: *"They only like me when I'm 'fine.'"* Your loved ones get the highlight reel, not the behind-the-scenes struggle. Another layer to this vicious cycle.

**Here's the truth bomb:** Vulnerability isn't weakness; it's **revolutionary courage**. Letting your cracks show isn't failing. It's an invitation for connection.

Try whispering *"I'm not okay. And that's human"* to someone who matters. That mask? It's negotiable. The real magic happens when you risk being seen.

# Smiling? No, I'm Drowning.

It's a quiet ache that takes root. One that leaves just enough energy to keep up the act, smiling through the cracks, while hollowing you out from within, day after day.

The things you once loved now feel hollow, distant. Everything that used to light you up feels meaningless. Your mind is overrun by toxic loops: *"You're worthless"*, *"You're a burden"*, *"You don't deserve help"*. Yet you keep performing "fine" like it's your full-time job.

You tell yourself no one could possibly get it, that this is just how things are now. That this dimmed-down version of you is all that's left. But deep down, you know these destructive thoughts aren't yours. They never were.

That flicker of fight still left in you? The part reading these words, hoping they'll resonate? That's the real you. The voice that deserves to be heard, trusted, and cranked up to full volume.

Don't wait until your smile completely shatters before reaching out. Ready to understand what's really happening? Let's break it down.

Those empty *"It'll be okay"* speeches that everyone tosses your way? They bounce right off because depression builds walls nothing can climb.

Their clumsy attempts to "fix" you reveal how much they care. But sometimes that love stings, like you're failing them by not bouncing back.

Stop piling guilt onto your pain. Their fumbling often hides their own fear of screwing up.

Their efforts fall short because they're treating the symptoms while missing the deeper story. But here's what no one tells you: Depression's roots aren't always a single thorn you can yank out. Sometimes it's a tangled knot of biology (a gene that misfires), old wounds, and the weight of being human. Maybe you trace it to a specific trauma, or it might feel like fog rolling in from nowhere. That's okay. This isn't about blaming your past or your DNA, it's asking: 'What let depression grow here?'

*"I'm fine"*—a quiet lie from a voice that forgot how to speak.

Your agency stolen by something that once claimed to care. Unmourned grief for the life you lost. You need no perfect origin story. Start here: What eases the ache by 1% today? What sharpens it? Track these like clues. Healing begins in the mess.

Depression hijacks your brain with what psychologists call **"cognitive distortions"**, or mental shortcuts that twist reality to feed your pain.

In this state, your brain literally can't see nuance, hope, or possibility. That tunnel vision? It's not you. It's a symptom, as real as a fever during the flu.

But there are stolen moments of light: That playlist that briefly cracks your emotional armor. Scalding showers that jolt you back into your body. Petting a dog and feeling time freeze for just 10 seconds

These moments matter. They're proof your brain is still fighting for you, scrambling for footholds toward healing.

**So why does it still feel impossible?**

Here's the paradox: The more you fight depression, the deeper it digs in. Like thrashing in quicksand. Modern therapies reveal a counterintuitive truth: Healing starts when you stop warring with your pain.

Accepting that you're struggling isn't surrender. It's acknowledging your hurt without layering shame on top, without beating yourself up for not "getting better faster".

"I'm wired to bolt, it's automatic."

I crave a great love story, but the second things get real, I freak out.

Last night at that party, I met someone. We clicked, easy conversation, good vibes. For once, I thought "Maybe...". But nope. My brain went full doomsday mode. I bailed with some BS excuse.

Now I'm crying over my self-sabotage spiral (again). That voice whispering "You don't deserve happiness"? It's on 24/7 replay.

I've gotta stop treating myself like the enemy.

# Love vs Anxiety: When fear Hijacks connection

In relationships, anxiety, often born from fear of rejection or abandonment, can trap you in a cycle of insecurity. You obsess over whether they'll leave or love you "enough".

Sound familiar? Do you **shut down** to avoid rejection? Do you **cling tighter** to dodge abandonment?

These fears aren't flaws. They're souvenirs from your childhood, when love came either too freely (smothering you) or too conditionally (making you perform for it). Those early blueprints designed your entire approach to love.

Awareness is your power move. Naming these fears lets you build relationships that thrive on truth, not fear.

The goal? Connection where love isn't a performance. And suddenly, intimacy isn't something that threatens your safety, it becomes the place where you finally feel safe.

Rate these statements to understand your relationship patterns:

## Fear of Rejection:

How much does rejection anxiety hijack your relationships?
*Example:* Someone you like ghosts your text. What's your internal monologue?

☐ ☐ ☐ ☐ ☐ ☐ ☐ ☐ ☐ ☐

"They're probably busy. they'll text back later."

"They probably don't like me. I'm overthinking things again"

## Fear of Abandonment:

How terrified are you of being left?
*Example:* Your partner plans a night out without you. What's your knee-jerk reaction?:

☐ ☐ ☐ ☐ ☐ ☐ ☐ ☐ ☐ ☐

"Cool, I'll enjoy some me-time."

"Why don't they want me to come? Are they tired of me?"

## Emotional Independence:

How comfortable are you being alone without your partner's validation?
*Example:* A weekend solo, empowering or existential crisis?

☐ ☐ ☐ ☐ ☐ ☐ ☐ ☐ ☐ ☐

" I feel fine. I enjoy my alone time."

"I feel empty. I don't know what to do with myself."

## Communication Under Stress:

How well do you voice fears without spiraling?
*Example*: Bringing up a sensitive topic: do you freeze, fawn, or speak up?

☐ ☐ ☐ ☐ ☐ ☐ ☐ ☐ ☐ ☐

"I feel safe enough to bring it up."

"Too scared of their reaction. I'll keep it to myself."

## Self-Confidence in Love:

How secure do you feel in your relationship?
*Example*: You're both in front of the bathroom mirror, your partner stares a little too long at your reflection. What's your brain's hot take?

☐ ☐ ☐ ☐ ☐ ☐ ☐ ☐ ☐ ☐

"They must find me attractive today"

"Why are they staring? What's wrong with me?"

## Trust Factor:

How easily do you trust your partner?
*Example*: They come home late with a vague excuse, does your mind go detective mode?

☐ ☐ ☐ ☐ ☐ ☐ ☐ ☐ ☐ ☐

"They probably got held up"

"They're hiding something. I know it."

**Anxiety thrives in isolation. Together, you can face it head-on.**

It's not that you lack love or affection. But there's that nagging sense of dread, theses worst-case scenarios that creep into your closest moments, sometimes without you even noticing.

**To you**: Trust yourself. Trust your strength to push through the fear. Anxiety isn't a life sentence. It's a sign to speak up, to share openly, to listen deeply. And your partner? Believe it or not, they want to be your teammate, your safe harbor.

**For both of you:** Share the weight between you. Sharing it is how you lighten the load. Those honest conversations? They're master keys to the mental prisons we build ourselves. Yes, love alone won't cure anxiety. But love? It's rocket fuel for healing.

Together, you can rewrite the script. Create new rituals, shared breathing exercises, midday check-in texts, small gestures that say *"I'm here."* Real love means showing up for yourself and each other. It's choosing to fight for "us," not just against anxiety.

That daily choice to fight for "us"? That's where you'll find the courage to choose each other, fear by fear.

# How your partner can help you overcome anxiety

*Let's start with the DON'T list*

Let's get real: **Your partner shouldn't be your anxiety's personal assistant.** Their instinct to "fix" everything for you? It usually backfires. When they constantly handle situations that trigger your anxiety, it creates a vicious cycle. You end up feeling less capable of managing things on your own and instead of helping, this actually feeds your anxiety. It also piles unnecessary emotional weight on them, which can strain your relationship.

So what's the better approach? Encourage them to be your **anxiety workout partner, not your anxiety bodyguard.** They should support you through your fears, not shield you from them. Take that dreaded phone call: instead of dialing for you, have them sit beside you while you make it. Let them give you a pep talk beforehand and cheer you on afterward. Sometimes just having someone in your corner changes everything.

**Here's the bottom line: They're not your therapist, and their hovering isn't love.** Sure, they mean well when they try playing "savior" or wrapping you in bubble wrap. But this well-intentioned overprotecting actually handicaps your ability to cope independently. Worse, it creates an unhealthy dynamic where you become emotionally dependent on them for basic functioning. That's not partnership—that's emotional outsourcing.

**Your partner can be your reality-check partner when your brain goes into disaster-movie mode.** When anxiety spirals hit, talk through those "worst-case scenario" thoughts with them. They can gently challenge your catastrophizing, showing you that most situations have multiple possible outcomes not just the disaster your mind fixates on. By brainstorming these alternatives together, you'll start doubting those initial fear-driven "certainties". Over time, you'll realize the first scary thought isn't always the most likely or the only option worth considering.

**Your partner can be your breathing coach during anxiety flare-ups.** Practice deep breathing exercises together: Sit side by side, sync up on slow inhales and exhales, and let them guide you through techniques like 4-7-8 breathing (inhale for 4, hold for 7, exhale for 8). This focused practice calms your nervous system and gives anxiety less room to roar. Make it a regular ritual, it becomes a bonding experience that strengthens you both while managing the anxiety.

**Most importantly, your partner can serve as your "calm anchor" when anxiety tries to hijack you.** By staying grounded when you're overwhelmed, they show you that anxiety doesn't have to take the wheel. Their steadiness helps you pause, zoom out, and ask the golden question: *"Is this fear fact-based, or just my anxiety talking?"* That mental space? It's a game-changer for regaining control over your emotional reactions.

Love isn't meant to make you second-guess your worth with every silence.

Love isn't meant to make you overanalyze every syllable until you lose your grip on reality.

Love isn't meant to make you scavenge for proof you still matter.

**But here's what matters more:**

Love isn't a band-aid for your old wounds or a cure for your fears. The anxiety that lingers inside you? It doesn't define your ability to love or be loved.

You're not in this to heal. They're not here to save you. Love is where you learn slowly, stubbornly to trust. Not just them. But mostly yourself.

# Anxious Attachment

Anxious attachment turns love into a minefield of imagined threats. It's that relentless voice that twists every relationship into a desperate scramble for reassurance.

Every unanswered text feels like proof they're pulling away. Every quiet evening becomes evidence you're not enough. This endless overthinking drains you, turning love into a source of dread instead of joy.

And the ways you try to feel safe? They backfire. You blow up their phone. You demand to know where they are, who they're with. You scroll through their texts, hunting for "proof" to confirm your worst fears. Their rough day at work? You're sure it's because of you.



Your partner starts drowning under the weight of your anxiety. Hanging out with friends becomes a threat. Needing space? You hear *I'm leaving*. Your fear of abandonment becomes a self-fulfilling prophecy pushing them away inch by inch.

But that deep sensitivity you've been taught to fear is actually your superpower in disguise. The issue isn't your ability to love it's how you protect yourself that needs rewiring. And we're about to show you how.

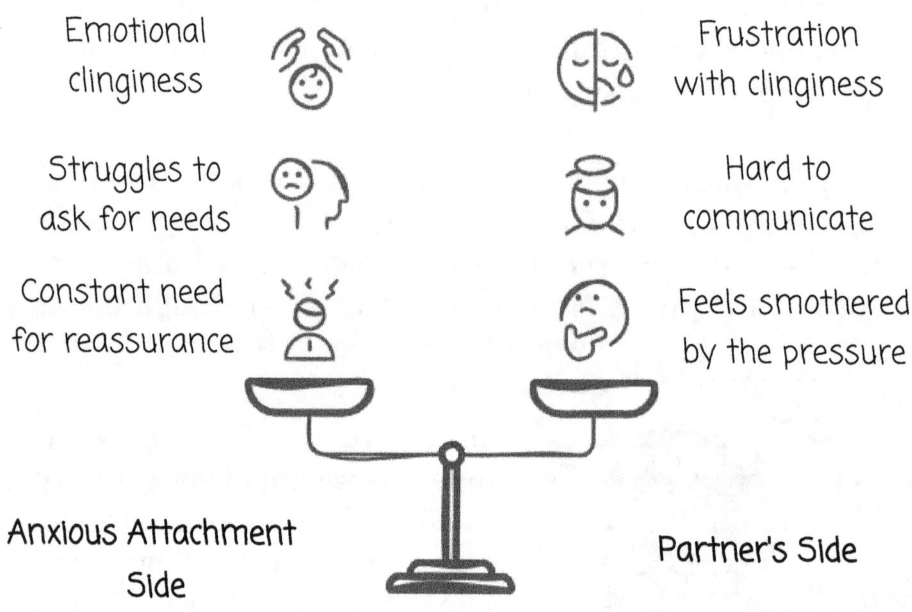


The Fragile Balance of Anxious Attachment in Relationships

# How to map your anxiety triggers

Anxious attachment is like a hypersensitive alarm system. To recalibrate it, you first need to understand what sets it off. This work happens in three steps: identify, understand, and transform.

**Step 1: Identify Your Triggers.** Here's a list of common situations that activate anxious attachment. Read carefully and note which ones hit home:

*In Communication:*

- A text left unanswered for hours
- That dreaded "read" receipt with no reply
- Shorter, less warm responses than usual
- Drop in messaging frequency
- A shift in their tone

*In social interactions:*

- Your partner laughing at someone else's jokes
- Them mentioning an ex or someone new with enthusiasm
- Their behaviour changing around other people
- Making plans that don't include you
- Visible chemistry with someone else

*In Relationship:*

- Sudden need for space or solo time
- Changes to established routines
- Arguments or disagreements
- Behaviors that remind you of past relationships
- Less initiative with shared plans

**Step 2: Track Your Reactions.** For each trigger you relate to, note:

- Anxiety intensity (1-10 scale)
- Automatic thoughts that pop up
- Instinctive reactions (controlling, withdrawing, confronting)
- How it affects the relationship

**Step 3: Connect the Dots.** Review your notes and look for:

- Triggers sparking the strongest reactions
- Most frequent fear-based thoughts
- Behaviors that make things worse

This awareness is your first step toward change. Once you understand what trips your anxiety wire, you can start building these strategies:

**With Your Partner:**

- Set clear communication routines (frequency, timing)
- Create a pre-approved reassurance list on your phone (written together)
- Agree on code words for rising anxiety
- Build comforting rituals (morning/night check-ins) that you can gradually phase out when you're ready

**For Yourself:**

- Cultivate activities that boost self-esteem
- Schedule fulfilling solo time
- Track your wins and progress
- Use past successes as proof you're resilient

"I've been chasing you so much, I've lost myself."
"Find yourself first, then you won't feel the need to chase me anymore."

# Are You the Puppet or the Author of Your Story?

The past is the blueprint for your present. Every memory, every experience, shapes how you react, choose, and connect today. It's a patchwork of joy and pain, wins and regrets that made you who you are. Take a moment and reflect:

**What emotion hits hardest when you revisit your past? Anger? Sadness? Fear? Something else?**

.................................................................

.................................................................

.................................................................

**What's your biggest regret right now? Does it haunt your current mindset?**

.................................................................

.................................................................

.................................................................

**How does that regret steer your choices or behavior today?**

.................................................................

.................................................................

.................................................................

**Are you clinging to resentment toward someone or something? How does that bitterness steal your peace?**

.................................................................

.................................................................

.................................................................

Could you forgive, and if not, what's standing in your way?

<br><br><br>

Can you spot moments where you acted against your values? How did that feel afterward?

<br><br><br>

When you think about your past, do you see yourself as a victim, a survivor or something else? Why?

<br><br><br>

How can you honor your past without letting it hijack your future?

<br><br><br>

What part of your past would you rewrite? And what's your plan to make that change real?

<br><br><br>

Your past is a part of you, but it's not the whole story. You can't rewrite yesterday but you can shape what comes next. Every sunrise is a new chance to pivot. To take what you've learned and build something stronger. Today and tomorrow are blank pages, waiting for your mark. Who you were doesn't define who you choose to become. So stand tall. Face the horizon with hope. And remember: every step you take today shapes the person you'll be proud of tomorrow.

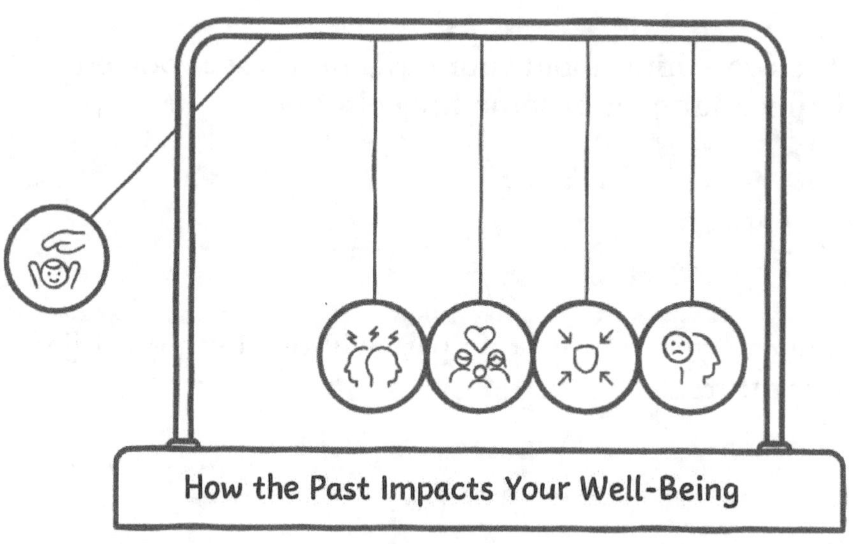


<table>
<tr><td>Childhood Experiences<br>Shape emotional development</td><td>Relationship Patterns<br>Affect how you interact with others</td><td>Family Beliefs<br>Guide life choices</td></tr>
<tr><td></td><td>Self-Criticism<br>Undermine self-confidence</td><td>Self-Criticism<br>Undermine self-confidence</td></tr>
</table>

# Old Wounds

Your old wounds still shape the way you move through the world—playing out the story of a child who had to grow up too fast. Crushed by expectations, haunted by the fear of disappointment, and starving for love that never came.

You feel those wounds in your sharp reactions, in how you harshly judge yourself and others, in that exhausting loop of reliving the same painful patterns.

Those shattered pieces, broken by the ones who should've protected you, taught you survival mode: smothering your needs and emotions, or anxiously scanning for the tiniest hint of rejection.

But today, those defenses don't serve you anymore. They cut you off from your true self or keep you chained to others' approval.

Your freedom starts when you choose to listen to your needs, not your fears.

These wounds shaped your story, but they're not who you are. They're unhealed chapters waiting for you to face them, heal them, and finally move forward.

# Connecting with your wounds

Set aside 20 minutes of quiet, uninterrupted time for this exercise:

1. **Recall a recent over-the-top reaction.** Write down the situation.

2. **Name the core emotion** you felt (anger, fear, sadness, abandonment...).

3. **Ask yourself these questions** and jot down your gut responses:

    - *"When have I felt this exact emotion before?"*

    - *"How old was I then?"*

    - *"What was happening back then?"*

    - *"What survival tactic did I develop to cope?"*

    - *"Is that tactic still helping me today?"*

4. **Write to your wounded inner self.** Start your letter with: *"I get why you had to protect us this way..."*

5. **End by offering a new approach.** Propose actions that fit the resilient adult you are now.

Repeat this whenever old triggers flare up. Over time, you'll spot destructive patterns faster and rewire them.

This exercise builds a real-world bridge between *awareness* and *action* with compassion, but no sugarcoating.

Dad, too cold to ever care,
Mom whose anger filled the air.
Between your wars and silent rage,
I learned survival at young age.

I believed for years it was me,
Something wrong I couldn't see.
Criticism took its toll
Deep within my soul.

Your blame, demands so high,
Stole my childhood, made me cry.
Perfect child who made no sound,
Tears swallowed, never found.

Your demons became my own,
Your pain the only life I'd known.
I thought perfection was the key
For you to finally love me.

Now I see your broken heart,
How your battles tore apart.
But understanding cannot heal
This pain I still feel.

I'm taking back
what's mine,
My right to simply
shine.

To love myself,
complete and free
Without your
permission to be.

# Original Wound

Missing love/validation
Rejection/Abandonment
No emotional safety
Having to earn love

## Limiting Beliefs

"I'm not worth it"
"I have to be perfect"
"Love comes with strings attached"
"I can't trust anyone"

## Defense Mechanisms

Always on emotional alert
Constantly testing relationships
Scared of commitment
Need to control everything

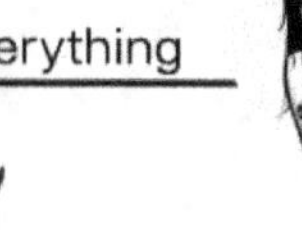

## Behaviors

Picking unavailable partners
Wrecking good relationships
Repeating family drama
Creating situations to fail

**Reinforcement**
Failed relationships, getting rejected over and over

Your past hardwired these survival responses. The same defenses that once saved you are now holding you back. Understanding them is how you take your life back.

Isn't it time to
put that down?
past

# Loneliness: That Sad Kind of Freedom

You've got a thousand followers but no one to call when your heart feels heavy. This loneliness, you wear it like a secret shame, inventing fake weekend plans when friends ask why you're free.

It's there when the last train drops you at your empty apartment, when you pass café terraces buzzing with laughter. It's there when you feel like an outsider in a crowded room, your words dissolving into air no one seems to breathe. Sometimes it whispers, *"They're all surface-deep, better off alone."* Truth is, you've just forgotten how to reach out.

But here's the irony: While you scroll endlessly in your dim-lit room, millions of others hide the same ache behind smiling selfies, too afraid to admit: *"I'm lonely."*

Yet those words, spoken aloud, might be the first step toward someone else waiting, like you, for silence to break.

So use those apps for what they're meant to be: a bridge to real people. Don't wait for the perfect crew. Build it: *"Tired of solo Sundays? Anyone up for brunch and a walk?"*

Real connection starts with awkward first steps, invitations sent with your heart racing. But that's the beauty: turning that loneliness into a hand reaching out and finding another hand reaching back.

Surrounded in body

Alone in soul

Real connection starts
when we dare to look up

# Overthinking

3 AM. You're staring at the ceiling, your mind racing, one thought dragging in another, spiraling into chaos.

Those thoughts that left you alone all day, when work drowned them out, now ambush you in the quiet. Sleep anxiety feeds insomnia, which feeds more anxiety. A brutal loop.

Here's the truth: Your brain is doing exactly what it's hardwired to do. For millennia, it's been a survival machine: analyzing, connecting, anticipating threats. It's a thought-generating engine. And the harder you fight those thoughts? The louder they scream.

What exhausts you isn't the thoughts themselves—it's believing them. Your mind throws out worst-case scenarios, and you treat them as gospel. You live them as absolute truths, not fleeting possibilities. They're just your brain's hypotheses, not prophecies. Understand that these are just thoughts produced by your mind, they don't define who you are. Next time you find yourself in this state, just try this:

# Play with Your Thoughts

This exercise has two parts: a playful way to lighten tough thoughts and a mindful method to observe them without getting overwhelmed.

## 1. Change the Tone of Your Thoughts

<u>Goal:</u> Make oppressive thoughts feel silly or absurd to drain their emotional power.

<u>Steps:</u> Identify a looping thought like *"I'll fail"* or *"I'm not good enough."*

Now play with it:

Stretch it out: Say it slowly, exaggerating every syllable, *"I'mmmm... goooing... to faaaail..."* The more exaggerated, the better.

Switch voices: Repeat it in a silly tone, robot, cartoon character, opera singer, etc.

Sing it: Use a tune you know (even a kids' song) and rewrite the lyrics: *"I might not succeed, but it's just a thought I don't need!"*

Notice the shift: Does it feel less heavy? Less believable? Playfulness creates distance.

## 2. Sort Facts from Fiction

<u>Goal:</u> Separate solid truths from your brain's dramatic storytelling.

<u>Steps:</u> Pick a stressful thought—like *"I suck at my job."*

**Split it into two columns:**

<u>Facts:</u> Observable, objective truths. What actually happened. Example: *"I missed a deadline."*

<u>Judgments</u>: All the drama and interpretation. What your brain added. Example : *"I'm incompetent and everyone thinks I'm useless."*

Reframe judgments: Add phrases like:

*"I notice I'm thinking..."*

*"I'm judging myself as..."*

Example: *"I notice I'm thinking I'll never improve."*

End with kindness. Remind yourself gently: *"This is just a thought—it's not me."*

**Why This Works:**

By bringing playfulness into your thoughts, you take away their seriousness. By checking facts, you begin to see how often your mind distorts reality.

And over time, you stop confusing your thoughts with the truth and start watching them with a little more distance, and a lot more compassion.

Don't think about that...
Stop thinking about it
At least try to think about it less
Think about something else!
Anything else!!
I'M TRYING!
You're driving yourself crazy!
I KNOW!!!

Here's an exercise to try next time negativity hijacks your mind: Follow the thread of a thought backward to uncover its origin and pinpoint the exact "tipping point" that sent you spiraling.

This practice shows how a single negative thought is often the tip of a chain reaction of interpretations and assumptions. By spotting that critical moment where your mind took a wrong turn, you'll learn to interrupt the chain earlier: stopping toxic thoughts before they snowball.

# The tipping point exercise

## 1. Trace the Thought Chain

**Identify your latest negative thought,** then dig into what came before:

*"What triggered this thought? What were you thinking about right before it?"*

**Work backward:** Keep asking yourself these questions after each answer to map the chain of thoughts that led to the negativity. Stop when you find the tipping point: the exact moment your mindset shifted from neutral/positive to negative.

## 2. Analyze the Shift

*"What caused this pivot?"*

Was it a physical sensation? An external trigger? A personality quirk? A past memory?

## 3. Question Your Assumptions

*"Could you have overanalyzed, misread the situation, or jumped to conclusions?"*

Challenge how you interpreted the triggering event.

## 4. Spot the Pattern

*"What does this reveal about your mental habits?"*

Note recurring themes in how you process stress or uncertainty.

## 5. Rewrite the Script

Now that you've traced it back and unpacked it, rewind to just before the tipping point. How could you redirect that initial thought in a healthier way?

Example:

Before: *"They're ignoring me."*

**Tipping point:** Assuming silence = rejection.

Redirect: "They might be busy. I'll check in later."

EXAMPLE :

**What's your latest negative thought?**

*"At the gym, I feel like everyone's staring at me and judging how I look."* *(Negative thought)*

**What triggered this thought? What were you thinking before?**

*"Right before that, I was thinking I might have gained some weight lately." (Another negative thought)*

**What triggered that thought? What were you thinking before that?**

*"My clothes felt a little tight." (Physical sensation)*

**And what were you thinking before that?**

*"I was planning my workout excited and ready to get back into fitness after a break." (Positive thought)*

**What do you think caused the shift?**

*"How my leggings felt."*

**Could you have misread the situation or jumped to conclusions?**

*"Maybe. The tightness made me assume others were judging me. Since I'm new back to the gym, I'm not used to how my workout clothes feel. I'm projecting my own insecurities—they're probably focused on their own routines."*

**What did you learn from this exercise?**

*"I spiral fast, assuming judgment from others when it's really my own self-criticism talking."*

**Rewrite the Script:**

*"Going back to when I felt motivated and happy about working out, I remember my goal was self-care and feeling strong. I'll focus on that energy and why I wanted to restart—not the noise in my head."*

Honor your effort,
Own your pride.

# Letter to Your Future Self

Fill this template with your own words—the letter you wish you could receive:

Dear [Your Name],

I know you're in the thick of one of life's hardest chapters right now. You're wondering if you'll ever feel truly happy or at peace. Here's the truth: You will.

You can't see it yet, but every _____________________ _____________________ *(current struggle or challenge you're facing)* is building you up, making you stronger. One day, you'll look back in awe at how far you've climbed.

You'll realize these__________________________ *(current hardships)* taught you priceless lessons. You'll learn to savor __________________________ *(small joys or moments),* to find peace in simple things. The battles you're fighting today are preparing you for a future where you'll feel more ______________________ *(a feeling or quality you want to develop).*

There'll be stumbles, but ______________________ _________________________ *(a positive perspective or lesson to learn from failure).* Every setback is just a coiled spring for your next leap forward.

Remember that moments of ___________________________

_______________________*(type of emotion or experience)*
are just as important as joyful ones. They give you the
chance to ____________________________ *(type of
reflection or action)*. Let them be part of your story, not the
whole book.

Every morning, you get to choose_______________
________________________________ *(action or choice)*.
This will lead to _________________________________

_________________________________________________

*(experiences or achievements)* you can't even imagine yet.

I'm proud of you for ___________________________
*(type of positive action or decision)*, even when quitting felt
easier.

You're far more ___________________________________
*(a positive quality)* than you know.

 Keep chasing _________________________________
*(your dreams, goals, or passions)*, that's how you'll build the joy
and calm you deserve.

**Your Future Self**

*(Who can't wait to meet you)*

"Why are we always chasing the next moment, as if it mattered more than the one we're in?"

# You. Here. Now.

The past haunts you. The future terrifies you. Those swirling thoughts in your head? They're just ghosts. The only moment where you can truly act, truly exist, is now. It's your lifeline when everything else crumbles.

Pause. Close your eyes. Feel the air filling your lungs, the ground beneath your feet, the rhythm of your heartbeat. These sensations anchor you to the only truth that matters: You're alive. Here. Now. Let this awareness become your sanctuary when negativity tries to drag you under.

Don't underestimate the power of this breath, this second. Right here, your fears lose their grip. Your regrets fade. This isn't magic, it's a muscle you can strengthen. Every time you return to the present, you starve anxiety of its oxygen.

You don't need hours of meditation or enlightenment. Freedom hides in the mundane: the bitter tang of coffee, a friend's laugh, sunlight warming your skin. It's in these ordinary moments that you gently reclaim your power— one grounded breath at a time.

Stay here a moment.

Everything else can wait.

# The Butterfly in Kuan Yin's Garden

*In Chinese mythology, Kuan Yin is the goddess of mercy and compassion. She embodies serenity and inner peace, teaching the importance of living with empathy and mindfulness in every moment.*

# The Butterfly in Kuan Yin's Garden

One day, an old monk, renowned for his wisdom, sat deep in meditation when his attention was drawn to a butterfly. Its dazzling wings fluttered endlessly, driven by a relentless quest for the next flower, the next sip of nectar, the next destination.

Curious, the monk rose and followed, letting the butterfly lead him through the garden, then beyond the monastery walls, until it finally settled in a sunlit meadow. Even there, its wings trembled, poised to chase some imaginary horizon while the flower beneath it offered everything it needed.

The monk smiled, recognizing in this dance the restless human mind. Like the butterfly, we spend our lives flitting from thought to thought, worry to worry, too frantic to see that the peace we crave is already here, in this single breath.

This story reminds us: Life isn't a race to rush through, always waiting for "better". Between who you were and who you long to be lies a sacred space: who you are. And it's here, in this stillness, that true transformation begins.

The past escapes you.
The future intrigues you.
The present belongs to you.

# Anxious Perception vs. Reality

| *Anxious Perception* | *Reality* |
|---|---|

"What if I make the wrong choice?"

"I'm trying something new."

"What if I don't like it?"

"I don't like it."

"I can't undo this."

"I make another choice."

"It's too risky, too uncomfortable."

"I've learned from my first decision."

*Imagined Consequence*

*Actual Consequence*

"I'll be trapped in a situation I hate, with no escape."

**"I'll adapt and find solutions."**

**"I'll reassess and adjust my path."**

**"I grow through the experience."**

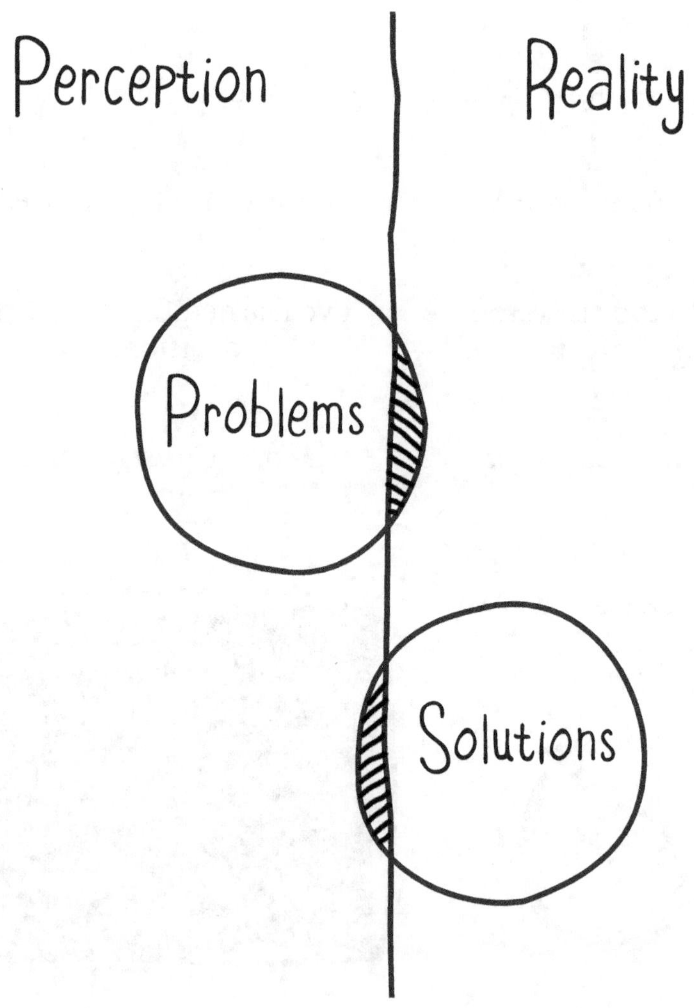


Perception
Reality
Problems
Solutions

# Living with Generalized Anxiety

Living with generalized anxiety is like carrying a backpack stuffed with stones, each one representing a worry, a doubt, a fear. Unlike passing anxiety, it follows you everywhere: rereading a text ten times before hitting send, catastrophizing about loved ones' safety, dreading every drive like it's a ticking time bomb.

You're stuck in constant red alert mode, scanning your surroundings for threats, real or imagined. That exhausting hypervigilance turns minor setbacks into mountains of worry, tiny doubts into endless mental loops.

But those stones weighing you down? You can set them free, one by one. Start with the smallest ones: breathe deep when panic surges, build grounding routines like a morning walk or a calming playlist, track your daily wins no matter how tiny they seem. This journey begins with micro-steps.

And you don't have to carry that backpack alone. Share the load with a friend who listens without trying to fix you, or a therapist who can help you sort which stones to keep and which to ditch.

Every stone you remove is proof you're stronger than your anxiety. Every step forward shows that change is possible, even if it's just one breath, one hour, one day at a time.

# The generalized anxiety loop

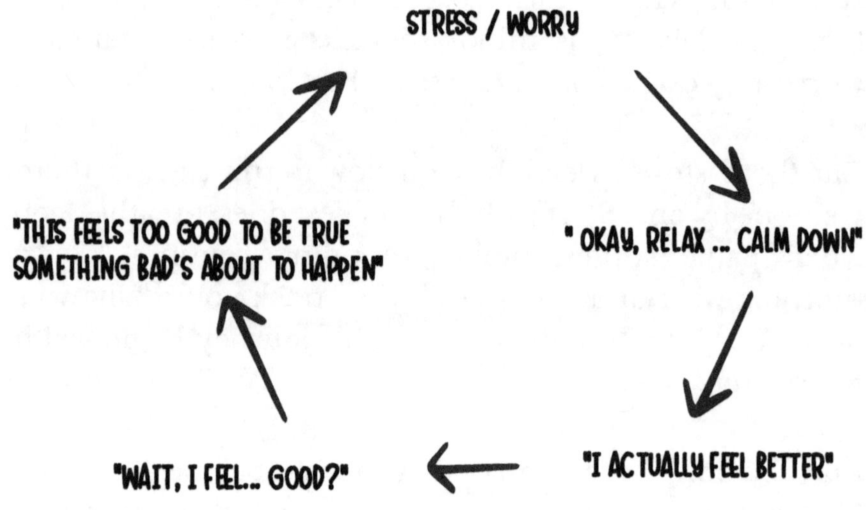

# Mid-Panic Attack

When panic hits, minutes stretch into hours and it feels endless. But like any thunderstorm, panic attacks always pass.

Your body isn't betraying you. Those intense sensations: sweating, shaking, struggling to breathe are its clumsy attempt to protect you from a threat it believes is real. The problem isn't your body's response; it's the misfire of your survival instincts.

Panic attacks drain you, but they're not dangerous. They won't make you lose control (even though it feels that way). They won't make you "go crazy". And they always end, no matter how long they seem to last.

What truly terrifies you isn't the symptoms, it's the fear itself:

Fear of feeling fear
Fear of losing control
Fear of being judged

Learning to ride out a panic attack means learning to trust your body. Even in the eye of the storm, a part of you remains anchored: steady, capable, and unbroken.

Here are some simple tools to help you find calm when the storm rolls in.

# Quick Tips to Calm a Panic Attack

**Activate your sense of temperature (thermoception):** Use cold to refocus your brain: a cold water bottle, ice cubes on your neck, or blasting the AC in your car. The goal is to shift your attention to a strong physical sensation.

**Engage your sense of taste intensely:** Suck on a lemon slice, vinegar pickles, sour candies, mint, or something salty. Just like with cold, the strong taste hijacks your brain's attention and grounds you in the moment.

**Check the time and remind yourself this won't last.** Mentally anchor yourself in the fact that the episode is temporary. Think about something soothing you'll do afterwards: a warm bath, a piece of chocolate, or anything comforting. Focus on positive thoughts—whatever you know will bring relief.

**Fix your gaze on a single point for a few minutes:** Pick a neutral object in your environment and stare at it steadily. The idea is to block involuntary eye movement and anchor your attention. This helps interrupt the mental spiral of negative thoughts.

**Use the 5-4-3-2-1 technique:** Name 5 things you can see, 4 things you can touch, 3 things you can hear, 2 things you can smell, 1 thing you can taste. This is a simple but powerful grounding exercise that brings you back into the present moment.

**Breathe**

**Diaphragmatic breathing:** This deep-breathing technique uses your diaphragm to increase oxygen flow and reduce anxiety. Inhale slowly through your nose, letting your belly rise, then exhale gently while contracting your belly.

To practice it, place one hand on your chest and the other on your stomach. Your stomach should rise as you inhale, while your chest stays still.

**4-7-8 breathing:** Inhale for 4 seconds, hold your breath for 7 seconds, then exhale slowly for 8 seconds. This method is known for its quick calming effect.

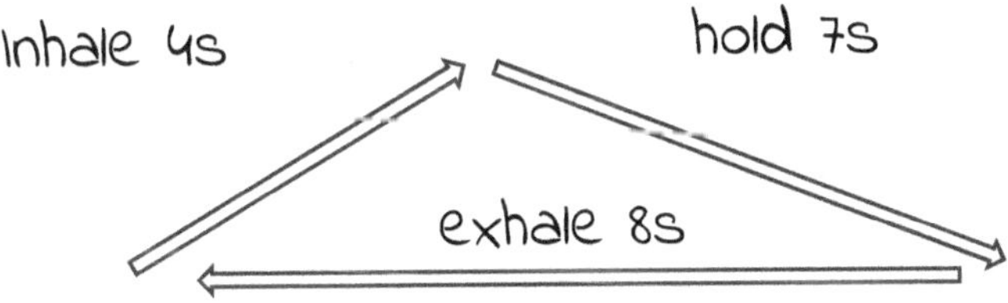


**Box breathing:** Inhale for 4 seconds, hold for 4 seconds, exhale for 4 seconds, then pause for 4 seconds before inhaling again. This technique helps focus your mind and ease anxious thoughts.

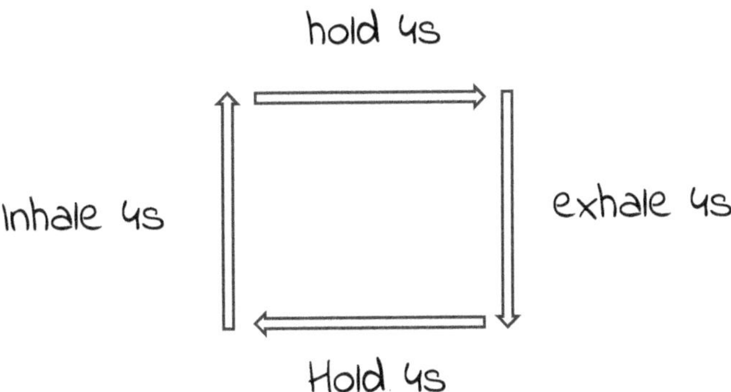

# Mapping Your Triggers

We usually react to what's on the surface—the panic attack itself—without seeing the underlying chain reaction that caused it. To understand and defuse these patterns, pay attention to:

### *BEFORE:*

- What was happening right before it hit? What were you doing?
- What was your emotional state already?
- What thoughts were running through your head?

### *THE TRIGGER:*

- What exactly tipped you over the edge?
- What meaning did you give it?
- What did you feel in that moment?

### *AFTER:*

- What was your first thought?
- How did you react?
- What did you do or avoid doing?
- What would you have done differently?
- What can you learn from this situation?

The goal isn't to judge your reaction, it's to understand the pathway that led there. This awareness becomes your early warning system. When you can identify your triggers, you can:

- See them coming without panicking about them
- Catch the warning signs early

- Create space between what happens and how you respond
- Build better coping strategies

Write down what you notice. Over time, patterns will emerge, giving you the keys to transform automatic reactions into conscious choices.

# Long-Term Wellness Strategies

**Exercise** is way more than just moving your body, it's a mood-regulating powerhouse. Not naturally athletic? No sweat. You don't need to become a gym rat overnight. The secret is starting ridiculously small. Ever heard of the Kaizen method? It's all about tiny, gradual changes that create lasting impact.

Applied to fitness, this means starting with baby steps: maybe a five-minute walk or some gentle stretches when you wake up. The goal isn't performance, it's pleasure. Movement should feel like self-care, not a punishment. Over time, your mind and body will start craving it.

Exercise is also your natural pharmacy for endorphins (those feel-good chemicals) and stress relief. Even just a few minutes daily is a huge win for your mental health, that's progress.

**Food** plays a bigger role in your mood than you might think and we're talking way beyond just "eating healthy". Some foods literally boost your brain chemistry.

- Boost serotonin, your brain's mood-regulating hormone, by eating foods rich in tryptophan like eggs, nuts, seeds, cheese, and fatty fish.
- Get your magnesium fix—found in spinach, almonds, and yes, dark chocolate—for better sleep and stress resilience.
- Try plant-based helpers like Rhodiola or saffron supplements, known to support emotional balance naturally.

On the flip side, limit caffeine and sugar bombs (sodas, candy) which can spike your energy, then drop you into irritability and fatigue.

**Sunlight** is nature's antidepressant. Even moderate sun exposure boosts vitamin D production, which is crucial for mood and overall health. Natural light also helps regulate your internal clock, improving both sleep and mental state. Just a few minutes outside can noticeably lift your spirits.

**Rest** isn't just about nighttime sleep, it's about giving your mind and body recovery time throughout the day. Struggling with insomnia? Try deep breathing, guided meditation, or calming bedtime routines. Power naps are underrated too: short and sweet, they can recharge your batteries without messing up your sleep schedule.

**Reconnect with what you love:** Passions aren't extras, they're emotional anchors. Whether it's painting, playing music, gardening, or something uniquely yours, creative outlets give your mind space to breathe. They build confidence, calm, and joy—essential tools for emotional resilience.

**Explore Gentle Alternatives**

There are many complementary therapies that support mental wellness. Try what feels right for you:

- **Kinesiology:** Movement to release emotional blocks
- **Herbal medicine:** Plant-based healing for balance and calm
- **Hypnotherapy:** Accessing the subconscious to shift patterns
- **Acupuncture:** Rebalancing energy via pressure points
- **Aromatherapy:** Essential oils like lavender or bergamot to soothe stress
- **Yoga:** Stretch, breathe, and reconnect with your body
- **Reflexology:** Targeted touch to calm the nervous system
- **Sophrology:** Breathwork and visualization to regain calm
- **Meditation:** Cultivating present-moment awareness

Each one is a path. Choose the one that speaks to your needs and commit to giving yourself that care.

You don't find happiness, you create it

# Identify Your Core Beliefs

Ever wonder why you react intensely to certain situations? Why some things trigger you more than others, or why you're drawn to specific people while avoiding others? The answer usually lies in your core beliefs—those automatic assumptions and perceptions that shape how you see and navigate the world.

Think back to a recent moment when your emotions were running high, maybe even overwhelming. Really put yourself back in that scene. Picture everything—the setting, the people, the whole vibe. Tap into how intense those feelings were, then answer these questions:

What words describe **ME** in that moment?

What labels did I assign **OTHERS**?

How did I view the **WORLD?**

Now look at what you wrote. What do you think? Does this really capture who you are, or does it reflect a distorted view of yourself or the world?

Do you apply these beliefs to EVERY situation? If not, what does that reveal?

Ask yourself whether these beliefs and perceptions are actually helpful and constructive. Are there parts of these convictions you could challenge or shift to create a more positive and balanced outlook on life?

# "I'll Do It Later... Tomorrow... Someday... Just Not Right Now"

Procrastination isn't really about being lazy, it's usually emotional escape in disguise. Part of you knows what needs to get done, but the scared part keeps winning the argument.

Behind every *"I'll do it later"* is often an unspoken *"I can't handle this right now"*.

Social media, binge-watching, video games: these aren't random choices. Your brain weaponizes them to avoid discomfort while pulling a double con: exaggerating how hard the actual task will be and overselling how good the escape will feel.

But there's a cost to all this avoidance: guilt piles up like unpaid bills, and progress stalls across every area of your life.

Break the cycle with micro-actions: Write down the task to make it real. Slice it impossibly small. Schedule it with brutal specificity. Then start before you feel ready, because action creates momentum, not the other way around.

When you face the thing—even clumsily—you'll discover this truth: You're stronger than your anxious brain claims. Every small step isn't just progress, it's proof that fear's grip on your life is loosening.

# Not-To-Do List

1. Don't postpone your happiness.
2. Don't isolate yourself.
3. Don't tie your happiness to material things like money – or immaterial ones like follower counts.
4. Don't ignore your own needs and emotions.
5. Don't constantly compare yourself to others.
6. Don't neglect the importance of self-care.
7. Don't stay in toxic relationships or situations.
8. Don't be afraid to ask for help or support when needed.
9. Don't set unrealistic or rigid expectations for yourself.
10. Don't forget to celebrate small wins and moments of joy.

# Understanding Your Emotional Range

Every emotion, whether joyful or painful, is part of your wholeness. The real challenge isn't to control them, but to welcome them without drowning in their waves.

The key?

Listen to what they're trying to tell you. Your anger might speak of a boundary crossed, your sadness of a need to be heard, your fear of a longing for safety. When you meet them without judgment, you uncover the map to your inner world.

The more you learn to recognize and accept your emotions, the more authentic your relationships become. No more pretending everything's fine or hiding what you truly feel. This honesty with yourself becomes your anchor: a strength that steadies you through life's storms.

Emotions aren't "good" or "bad". They're signals from within, pointing to what needs your attention. To ignore them is to cut off a part of yourself. To listen, even when it's uncomfortable, is to choose full aliveness, aligned with who you truly are.

# Decoding Your Emotions

**Sadness and anger** both map the distance between what is and what could be. Sadness blooms from loss or unmet longing—whether it's grief, heartbreak, or a need that's been quietly aching inside you. Anger flares when boundaries get crossed, when your values clash with reality, or when wounds are screaming to be heard. **Both emotions reveal the gap between what you accept and what you resist.**

These feelings aren't flaws—they're your inner compass. Sadness points you toward what you need to feel whole again, while anger shows you what's worth defending to stay true to yourself. Their power lies not in how intense they feel, but in what they reveal about your deepest needs.

**Doubt, uncertainty, helplessness**—these shadows creep in when you're facing the unknown, usually from fear of making the wrong move rather than lack of options. **What paralyzes you isn't the choices themselves, but the distrust in your own judgment.**

Don't let fear of missteps freeze you. These moments of doubt are invitations to explore why you question yourself so deeply. Every shaky step still moves you forward. And sometimes, right in the thick of uncertainty, your greatest strengths emerge—if you dare keep walking despite the tremble in your bones.

**Envy and jealousy** flare when you measure your life against others', feeling left behind or less than. Envy makes you want what they have; jealousy makes you panic about losing what you already have. **These emotions reveal less about others and more about your own unmet needs and hidden fears.**

Instead of sideways glances, focus on your own path. Your struggles, growth, and victories belong solely to you. Comparison is a game no one wins, every person you envy fights battles you can't see.

**Guilt and shame**, both speak to mistakes, but in radically different voices. Guilt says *"I did something wrong"*, while shame claims *"I am wrong"*. They often crush you unfairly. Guilt gnaws at you for things beyond your control: a loved one's pain, others' moods, situations you can't change. You end up carrying the world's weight. Shame goes deeper, making you question your very worth. These aren't helpful guides, they're parasites feeding on your anxiety.

Toxic guilt even taints your successes, leaving you wondering if you deserve them and over-apologizing for simply existing. Learn to spot when guilt stems from anxiety rather than actual missteps. You're not responsible for everyone's happiness, and you have the right to exist without constant remorse.

**Solitude and isolation** live in that space between you and others, a gap that's sometimes chosen, sometimes forced on you.. Isolation can make you feel invisible, disconnected from a world moving without you. These feelings aren't always signs of weakness or social failure; sometimes it signals hunger for deeper, more authentic  connection. In those quiet moments, you might find unexpected clarity or peace. But when the weight grows heavy, remember you can reach out by sharing passions or offering small kindnesses. Solitude nurtures growth, but human bonds add richness that solitude alone never can.

There's No Manual for Suffering

There's no manual for pain, no timeline for healing.

No "right way" to suffer.

Some hurl their anguish into the world, others whisper it,
many hide it away.

Let no one tell you what you should feel. They don't live
in your body. They don't carry your scars.

Tend to that hurting part of you. It only asks to be heard.

Every step matters, even the smallest, even those that
circle back. Healing isn't a straight line.

You hold a soundless strength within you, an unadvertised
courage.

Own it.

# The Weight of Choice

We all have choices—but choosing means letting go.

That dread that rises when you decide, that voice whispering you'll get it wrong again, replaying every past "mistake". Others seem so certain, so decisive, while you dissect every option into exhaustion.

*"What if...?"*

But truth is: There's no perfect path. Every door closed opens another. Every "no" is a "yes" to yourself. Every release is freedom wearing unfamiliar clothes.

You don't have to carry the ghost of every road untaken. You can't live a thousand lives at once. This tormenting indecision? It might be your integrity refusing easy answers.

Pause. Listen, not to the voice that judges, doubts, or compares, but to the one deep within that knows. The one that feels. The one that guides.

The only real choice is the one that keeps you true to yourself, even when it means disappointing others' expectations.

"Ever heard of high sensitivity?"

Why do I suddenly want to cry?
This is so stupid to react like this!
If I don't answer he's going to be mad
at me... He thinks I'm too emotional!
And if I answer wrong, he'll take it
personally... I'm sure my face is
all red right now, great!
If I tell the truth, he's going to
think I'm weird...

"Uh... A little..."

# Highly Sensitive & Completely Drained

Other people's emotions hit you as if they were your own. Their joy lights you up; their pain tears you apart. The world always feels too much, too loud, too intense, too in-your-face.

Where others shrug off criticism, you replay it until it makes you physically sick. Yet this sensitivity is also your superpower, you read subtle cues and unspoken truths in a heartbeat.

And it drains the life out of you...

Here's what you need to understand: feeling others' pain doesn't mean you must fix it. Yes, you're an empath. Yes, you have a huge heart. But the world's weight isn't yours to carry.

Question your interpretations too. That urgency around others' emotions, that belief everything depends on you, that's not always reality talking. Others have their own journey, their own strength.

This hypersensitivity lets you live with a depth and authenticity most never experience. Protect this tender part of yourself. It doesn't need fixing, just safeguarding.

Your exhaustion isn't weakness. It's your soul's witness to everything you've carried.

High Sensitivity

Advantages   VS   Drawbacks

| Advantages | Drawbacks |
|---|---|
| Deep emotional connection | Emotional overload |
| Quick understanding of subtleties | Chronic fatigue |
| Authentic living | Over-interpreting others' needs |
| Empathy | Burden of responsibility |
| Emotional depth | Risk of emotional burnout |

**Turn Sensitivity into Strength:**

Learn to spot the exact moment your nervous system tips into overload—when sounds suddenly sharpen into knives, when light touches feel like invasions, when others' emotions surge through you like a rising tide.

To regulate this constant overstimulation draining your system, start tracking your saturation level on a 1-10 scale throughout the day. Note the physical warnings: jaw clenching, stomach knots, shallow breathing.

Once you recognize these signals, you shift from reactive to strategic. That meeting tomorrow? You know it'll tax your system, so you arrive early to claim quiet space, choose seats near exits, and schedule non-negotiable recovery breaks.

Your sensitivity rewires how you navigate environments. Open offices become energy maps to traverse mindfully. Social interactions turn into carefully metered exchanges. Time splits between engagement periods and essential recovery phases.

You reframe withdrawal needs not as weaknesses, but as biological imperatives. Like an athlete balancing training and rest, you alternate social connection with recharging solitude, because high-performance humans honor their operating limits.

Here's how to create that balance in three simple steps:

1.  **FEEL IT OUT**
    - Notice what's actually happening in your body
    - Take in what you're sensing without judging it
    - Get specific about those physical sensations
    - Let your emotions do their thing without shutting them down

2.  **FIGURE IT OUT**
    - Make sense of what you're feeling—don't rush it
    - Sort out what's yours versus what's coming from around you
    - Connect the dots between what you feel and what's happening
    - Give yourself space to think it through

3.  **DO SOMETHING ABOUT IT**
    - Pick your response instead of just reacting on autopilot
    - Say what you need to say in a way that works
    - Take action based on what you've figured out
    - Take care of yourself and respect what you need

This isn't a one-and-done thing—it's more like a cycle. You'll need to hit pause regularly to check back in with yourself, switch between speaking up and stepping back, and keep balancing thinking with doing.

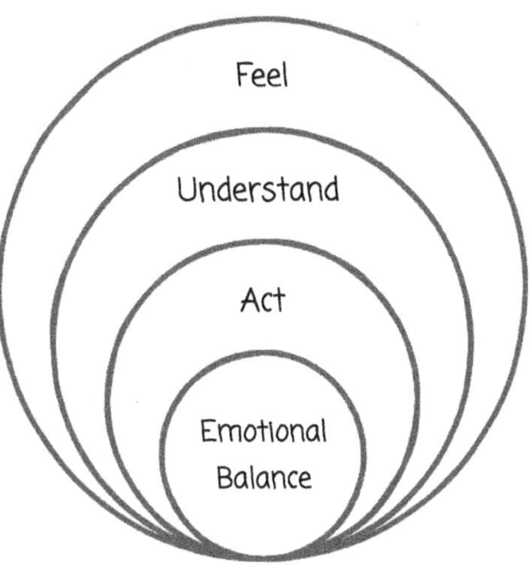

## The Lonely Depth of Being Highly Sensitive

The hardest part of being highly sensitive is the constant disconnect. That feeling of moving through a parallel world where everything hits harder, cuts deeper, pulses brighter. Others' confusion isn't just awkward, it's a daily bruise that widens the gap between you and everyone else.

When people call you "too much", they don't understand: you're not overreacting, you're deeply feeling. How can you explain that your responses aren't excessive, just authentic to the intensity of what you experience? Faced with this constant misunderstanding, their confusion teaches you to shrink, to dull your reactions, to wear a mask.

Here's the cruel twist: this sensitivity makes you exquisitely empathetic. You read people with uncanny precision, anticipating needs before they're even spoken. Yet this very gift—the thing that connects you so deeply to others— leaves you feeling profoundly misunderstood.

**Stop trying to be less sensitive. Start mastering how to inhabit it.** In a world obsessed with surface noise, your sensitivity is quiet rebellion. It lets you see behind facades, feel what others tune out completely. Don't let their confusion define you. Instead, use it as a mirror to reveal the depth of your soul and the richness of who you are.

# WHEN WAS THE LAST TIME YOU DID SOMETHING FOR THE FIRST TIME?

If you're drawing a blank, it's time to ask yourself: when will you finally step out of your comfort zone? Break the routine! Life is built from moments we collect. Every new experience is fuel to grow, learn, and thrive. Push yourself. Dare to surprise yourself. Live. The world is brimming with opportunities.

What if today's the day?

# You Have Every Right

Read each statement and check it off if you've felt or done this recently. This isn't about judging yourself—it's about recognizing that these things are totally normal parts of life.

☐ I changed my mind when I saw things differently.

☐ I took my time because moments matter.

☐ I felt scared because that's what happens when facing the unknown.

☐ I messed up and got stronger because that's how we learn.

☐ I wanted different things than the people around me, and that's okay.

☐ I made a mistake and decided to learn from it.

☐ I disagreed with someone because my opinion matters.

☐ I did something just for me because I deserve to enjoy life my way.

☐ I asked for help because knowing when you need support is actually smart.

☐ I felt like an outsider and decided that being different is pretty cool.

☐ I said *"I don't know"* because pretending to be perfect is exhausting.

☐ I let someone down and realized I can't make everyone happy all the time.

**How does it feel to own these parts of yourself?**
**What does this tell you about handling life's messiness?**

# Quiet the Bad, Listen to the Good

So let's check in for a second. How are you doing with yourself? Going through this book, you might have noticed some changes, even small ones.

Look at this list. Any of these improvements sound familiar? Check the ones that fit.

☐ I trust myself more.

☐ I stay calm easier.

☐ Things with my family and friends are better.

☐ My daily routine feels more balanced.

☐ I'm back to doing things I actually enjoy.

☐ I sleep better.

☐ I'm okay with who I am.

☐ I talk to people more.

☐ I actually enjoy my days.

☐ I'm more chill.

☐ People say I seem better.

☐ I smile without forcing it.

☐ Work doesn't stress me out as much.

☐ I feel thankful more often.

☐ Arguments don't freak me out.

☐ The future doesn't scare me as much.

Other changes you've noticed:

These are proof you're growing, signs that you're becoming the person you want to be.

Some days might feel like nothing's different. That's totally normal. Change doesn't always show up right away. But if you checked even one thing, something's working, something's shifting.

And if you didn't check anything today, that's fine too. Just knowing where you want to go is already progress.

Think of this book as your starting point, not your destination. Keep it around as long as you need it. When you're ready, set it aside and keep going. You've got everything you need to figure out your own happiness. You can do way more than you think.

**Show up for yourself**

| | |
|---|---|
| Trust yourself. | Go at your speed. |
| Every step matters. | Your path is yours. |
| Believe in your wins. | Celebrate the small stuff. |
| Be patient with yourself. | You're resilient. |
| Stop doubting. | Welcome what's new. |

Celeste Leroi

Life's full of those moments when you feel small, vulnerable, like everyone can see right through you. That's the kind of truth I wanted to explore in this book: a journey through the twists and turns of anxiety, self-worth, and the search for inner peace.

This book is my way of saying: You're not alone.

If this book helped you or touched you in any way, feel free to leave a review on Amazon. You can scan this QR Code with your phone:

Thank you for your support and kindness.

www.ingramcontent.com/pod-product-compliance
Lightning Source LLC
Chambersburg PA
CBHW051426150726
48000CB00005B/1975